The Flight

How My Family Outsmarted The KGB

Lev E. Perlov
Contributions By: Katy G. Meilleur

Copyright © 2024

All rights reserved.

All rights reserved. No portion of this book may be reproduced, stored in a retrieval system, or transmitted in any form or by any means; electronic, mechanical, photocopy, recording, scanning, or other, except for brief quotations in critical reviews or articles, without the prior written permission of the author.

Cover by: Mikhail Starikov

Literary consulting, editing, and formatting, by Clara Rose & Company.

Published by RoseDale Publishing
12100 Cobble Stone Drive, Suite 3
Bayonet Point, Florida 34667

ISBN-13: 979-8-9889895-4-7

This book is a true story based on the life of Lev E. Perlov and his family. The names and details of some individuals have been changed to protect their privacy.

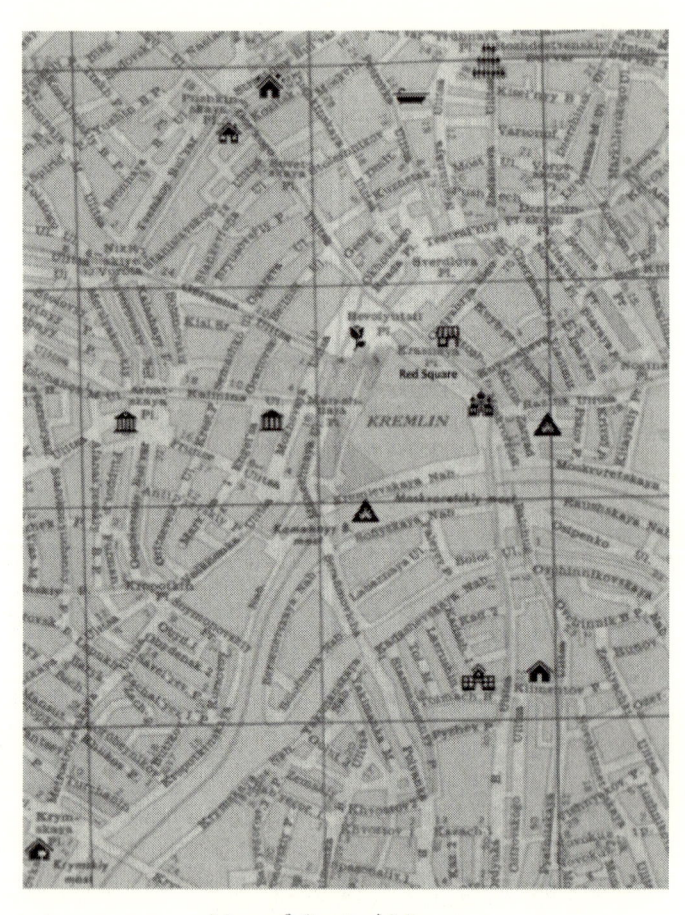

Map of Central Moscow

Legend for Map of Central Moscow

- Childhood home on Gorky (A.K.A. Tverskaya) Street
- Sisters' home on Kozitsky Lane
- Military school near Tretyakov Art Gallery
- Bombing sites during evacuation of military school
- Lenin library
- Sandunov public baths
- Stampede at Trubnaya Square for Stalin's funeral
- Home with first wife and daughter Emma
- Meeting place of Valentina, second wife
- Dutch embassy at Arbat Square
- Orphanage prior to military school
- St. Basil's Cathedral
- "G.U.M." translated "Main Department Store"

*All maps courtesy of Geography and Map Division,
U.S. Library of Congress*

Imagine!
Worlds beyond the sky,
or winged monsters fit to fly,
or reincarnation when I die,
or mountains millions of feet high.
Imagine these can I.

Imagine...
lessons that are taught
to someone who with tears has fought
and final glimpse of homeland caught
to gain the better lifestyle sought.
Imagine? I cannot.

By: Katy G. Meilleur

(Katya)

THE FLIGHT

A Dedication From Katy(a)

To my mother for her bravery and unwavering support of my father in the difficult, frightening, and momentous decisions in this story that ultimately changed the course of my life. I thank her for being a risk-taker. It was a joy to walk down memory lane with her and recall the astounding twists and turns that led up to the moment of the flight.

THE FLIGHT

Table of Contents

Acknowledgments 5

Preface 9

Rough Start 19

After the War 31

Strapped for Cash 43

Unexpected Romance 57

Finding My Calling 71

Closer to Freedom 83

Saved by a Dream..93

The Subpoena 107

Leaving On A Jet Plane 121

Brave New World 133

Conclusion...143

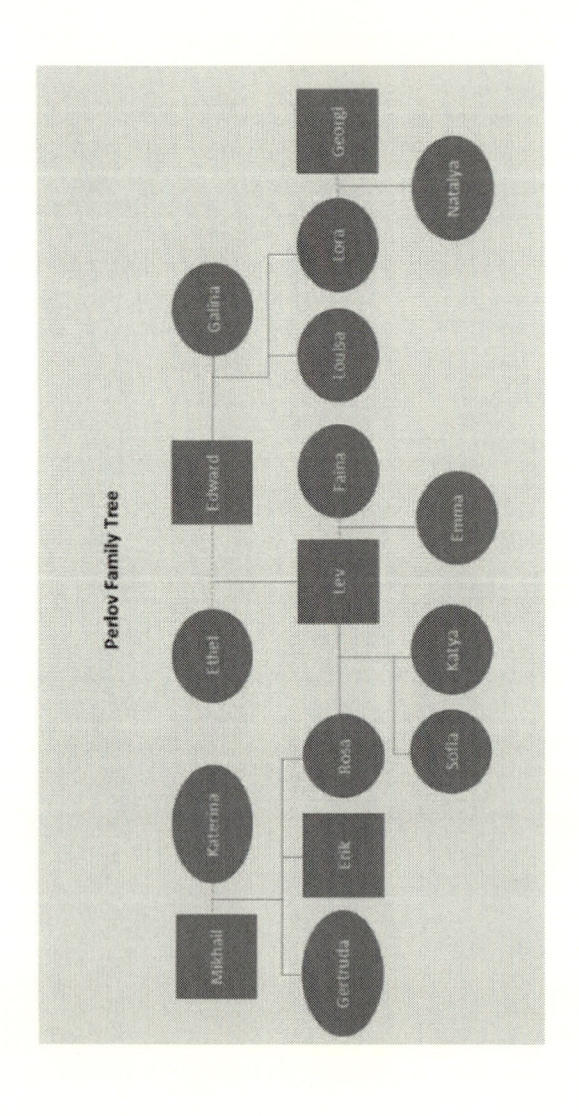

THE FLIGHT

Perlov Family Tree

THE FLIGHT

Acknowledgments

By Katy(a)

There are several people to thank who helped me publish my father's story. Given that the first half of his memoirs were in Russian and were about Soviet culture, which I have not personally experienced even though I was born there, I could not have done this without them.

To my half-sister Emma, for her immediate willingness to help with this project when I initially asked; and for sharing her translational and cultural prowess with me over many hours to help me clarify both linguistic and cultural idioms to make the meaning of Dad's words shine through into English. It was such a pleasure to collaborate with her on our dad's story and, in a small way, regain many years we did not have together. To Peter, Emma's son, for additional nuances in translation.

To my first cousin Natalya, Aunt Lora's daughter, for all the care with which she shared documents, stories, and bits of history about our grandfather and his second wife, her grandmother. For her consoling nature and expertise regarding the psychologically dark sequelae of this story in our lives. She is a

THE FLIGHT

treasure to me. To her daughter (also Katya), and her husband Alexey, who provided cultural context for me over many hours of discussion.

To my Aunt Louisa, for sending me her own memoirs and her mother's to make sure I got the details correct in publishing my father's story. What a gift to know my father's two half-sisters, albeit later in life, and to share a common family story with them.

To my parents' friend and mine, Alina, who encouraged me to pursue this idea and who faithfully read the chapters that required translation to make sure they were true to my father's original writing. For her love and support.

To my friend, Vladimir, Oscar's son, for confirming the details about his father's involvement in the escape, as his father is no longer with us, and for clarifying the language around those events. Although he has likewise passed, I will always be grateful to Victor for helping my dad when he needed it most at great cost to himself, and by extension the same thanks to his deceased wife Sophie, and their family.

Thank you to my husband, Phil, and children, Mathieu and Eve, who gave me the freedom, time and space to complete this project. I deeply love and appreciate each of them.

THE FLIGHT

Lev's father, Edward,
at the Black Sea, 1930

THE FLIGHT

Galina, Lev's stepmother, prior to Akmolinsky Labor Camp for Wives of Traitors to the Motherland, Moscow, circa 1935

THE FLIGHT

Preface

By Katy G. Meilleur
(Katya)

It was a snowy, cold, winter night in Moscow when my mother went into labor with me. It was January of 1973, and no taxis would take my parents to the hospital for fear my mother would deliver me in the cab. Finally, one taxi driver took pity on my parents and drove them in the nick of time. I was born at the hospital "en caul", a rare event when the mother's water does not break; I entered the world inside an intact amniotic sac.

"She's born with a veil, what a sign of good luck!" proclaimed the midwife to my mother. (In those days, fathers were not allowed in the delivery room.) Seven months later to the day in August 1973, my family would narrowly escape the Soviet Union.

This is the story of my family's escape, which my father penned in his own words before his passing in 2006. Given the times we are living in now, when immigration into the U.S., the Russian Ukrainian war, and the Gaza-Israeli conflict are pressing issues, it seemed apropos for me to curate and publish my father's memoirs.

First, I think it is important to showcase that many immigrants still make up the backbone of America. Our success contributes to the overall success of our

THE FLIGHT

country of naturalization. Based on personal experience, not only of my own immigration but also that of my husband from Canada, I agree wholeheartedly that it is critical to update the process of immigration in the U.S. It is very cumbersome. However, we do not need to throw the baby out with the bathwater and fear immigrants altogether.

Second, my father's story is timely because the fragility of democratic nations and societies has come to light recently. Countries where freedoms are allowed and supported, such as freedom of speech, press, and religion, seem now remarkably fragile. Promoting the truth that all people are created equal, as stated in our Declaration of Independence, and restraining the dangers of ethnic superiority (racism) are also the responsibilities of democratic nations.

My father loved and memorized the Declaration of Independence. I remember him spontaneously reciting it to me once as a young child. During a bedtime routine, he suddenly burst out with "We hold these truths to be self-evident, that all men are created equal, that they are endowed, by their Creator, with certain unalienable rights, that among these are life, liberty, and the pursuit of happiness." His story is a call to take note of how to be responsible as individuals for our precious freedoms lest they disintegrate, and we find ourselves living in a society like the one my father grew up in.

My father was born in Moscow too, albeit 47 years

THE FLIGHT

earlier than me, in December of 1926. It was a chaotic time on the heels of several major events in Russian history: the Revolution (1917), the civil war between the Reds (Bolsheviks) and the Whites (anti-Bolsheviks) (1918-20), the formation of the Soviet Union (1922) under the leadership of Vladimir Lenin, and the rise of Joseph Stalin after Lenin's death in 1924.

Into this incredibly tumultuous era, he was born. As a very young boy up to the age of 6 years, he grew up on Gorky Street in the heart of Moscow, just south of its intersection with Pushkin's Square. This street, named after the Russian author, Maxim Gorky, bustled with people going to and from its restaurants, bakeries, meat and produce stores, specialty shops, and telegraph and postal services. He felt its vibrancy as a boy. To this day, it remains a main street in Moscow, with the bottom of its hill culminating in the heart of Moscow: the Red Square, Kremlin, St. Basil's Cathedral, and the famous shopping mall, "GUM" or "Glavny Universalny Magazin," translated "the Main Department Store." After the collapse of the Soviet Union, Gorky Street was renamed Tverskaya Street.

My father's parents met outside of modern-day Russia. My father's father, Edward, was born in 1899, likely in Vienna. According to family legend, he moved to Russia at the age of 19 after getting into a fight at a bar with a drunk man who was bothering a young woman. To defend her, he punched the guy. Being quite strong, Edward accidentally killed him in the act. Upon further family research, however, he was listed

THE FLIGHT

in Austrian records as a prisoner of war of Russia after World War I. Either way, he stayed in Russia to become part of the Revolution as he believed in the ideals of communism at that time. He became a member of the communist party in the U.S.S.R. just as he had been in Austria.

In Western Ukraine, which was then still part of the Austro-Hungarian empire, he met my grandmother, Ethel, a nurse, and moved to Moscow. Once there, he changed his surname to Perlov and picked up a patronymic according to Russian tradition, which is essentially a middle name based on your father's first name. Therefore, in the U.S.S.R. he went by Edward Rudolphovich Perlov. My father was an only child. By the time he was approximately 5 years old, in 1931, Edward decided my grandmother was unbearable to live with due to mental health issues. My grandparents divorced. Ethel's mental health declined further after the divorce, but Lev remained with his mother.

Edward was part of a trade union and worked as a supervisor in a trade. He was well-educated but, because he was raised in Austria, he spoke Russian with a German accent. Not long after leaving my grandmother, he got married again to a Russian aristocrat named Galina. They lived on Kazitski Lane near the Stanislavsky Theatre, across Tverskaya Street from my dad and his mother. They had two girls, my dad's younger half-sisters, Louisa, and Lora.

THE FLIGHT

According to my father and his side of the family, Galina was a beautiful, intelligent, well-educated, and talented woman. She was a chemical engineer, with a specialty in gold overlay of porcelain. She was also an extraordinary piano player. She had been a pupil of the famous composer Rachmaninov and a student at the Gnesinksy Conservatory. She and my grandfather enjoyed entertaining in their home. My dad frequented his father's second family to enjoy these get-togethers. As a child, he witnessed vigorous discussions in their Moscow apartment about politics and culture.

Despite this brief period of light and warmth, my dad experienced, the times gradually became very dark under Stalin. Throughout his reign from 1924 to 1953, many Russians came to live in fear. They knew that one wrong move or statement could be misinterpreted as dissent against "the State," which would endanger their lives.

Many were sent to harsh labor camps. The camps are known as the GULAG because they were managed by a department loosely translated as Main Department of Camp Management, which in Russian is abbreviated G.U.Lag. for "Glavnoye Upravleniye Lagerey". Because of this, Russians could not trust their neighbors or friends for fear of being turned in for anything they might say or do. Facts became irrelevant due to the absence of fair trials. More and more people were incriminated based on allegations alone. Stalin considered well-educated people, even those who

THE FLIGHT

were communists, a threat. He eradicated such people by sending them to the GULAG system or executing them in mass shootings in Moscow.

Sadly, during the Great Terror of Stalin, a ruthless purge that spanned from 1936-1938, my grandfather fell victim to one of the mass shootings in Moscow. In March of 1937, having been accused of being a traitor and a spy against the state, he was tortured and then shot to death at Butyrski Prison. Edward never met his daughter Lora.

Approximately one million other people were executed in Moscow or died in the GULAG camp system between 1936 and 1938 (Ellman EUROPE-ASIA STUDIES, Vol. 54, No. 7, 2002, 1151–1172). Years later, after Stalin died in 1953, they were officially cleared of treason and exonerated by the Soviet government. My grandfather and others had never actually committed any crimes against the state... the accusations for which he lost his life had been fabricated.

Later in the same year, 1937, Galina was also taken in the great purge. Louisa was 4 years old at the time and Lora was 7 months old and still breastfeeding. Initially, Galina served in Butirskaya Prison in Moscow. But approximately six months later she was sent to Kazakhstan, to a well-known labor camp called "ALZhIR" which stands for "Akmolinksiy Lager Zhon Izmennikov Rodiny" or, in English, "Akmolinsk Camp for Wives of Traitors to the Motherland."

THE FLIGHT

Because she was a proficient chemical engineer, Galina used her skills and oversaw the development of three factories in the labor camp. Due to her contributions, she was allowed to exit the territory of ALZhIR at times. She served in the labor camp for a total of about six years and then she was allowed to live only in Siberia for the following two years. Thankfully, Galina survived and returned to Moscow in 1948. Until then, Galina's mother took care of her girls.

Galina had hurt her hand in the GULAG while chopping firewood and could not play the piano professionally upon her return to Moscow. She was no longer registered as a resident in Moscow as required by law to live there. So, she stayed in Louisa's apartment, mostly hiding behind a wardrobe and leaving only at night. She passed away in 1992.

At the time of his father's death in 1937, my father was 10 years old. His mother had worked as a nurse at a Moscow hospital. After my grandfather's death, she decided she could no longer take care of my father and placed him in an orphanage in central Moscow near the Moskva River.

Even at that age, my father began to understand that, as the son of an accused enemy of the state, his future looked increasingly bleak. He stopped visiting his two younger sisters to protect them from any negative association with his last name as it was the same surname as their father's. In fact, soon after Galina's

THE FLIGHT

deportation to ALZhIR in Kazakstan, her mother switched Louisa and Lora's last names to hers. She also changed their patronymic to Alexandrovna, her husband's name, for the same reason. Acknowledging that one was a child of an accused enemy of the state was to be avoided at all costs.

After he was placed in the orphanage, my father became concerned about his future. And that's where he begins telling his story in chapter one.

THE FLIGHT

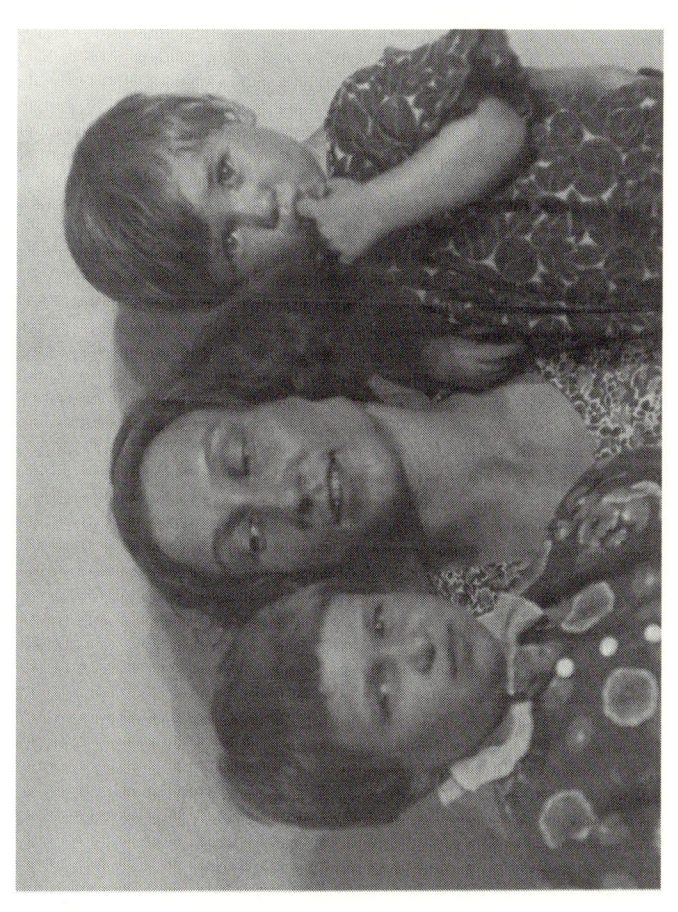

Louisa (left), Lora (right) and
their mother Galina's sister, Nina (center) Circa 1938,
after Galina was sent to ALZhIR in GULAG

THE FLIGHT

Lev, first row, second from right, First Moscow Specialty School of the Air Force, circa 1941

THE FLIGHT

Chapter One
Rough Start

I had just finished seventh grade at the beginning of June 1941. At that time, I was living and going to school in an orphanage in Moscow where my mother had been forced to send me two years earlier. We had no place to live then, she was unemployed, my father had been shot back in 1937, and we were destitute and disadvantaged. We were like millions of other Soviet citizens in that Stalinist paradise called the Soviet Union. I was fourteen years old at the time.

Usually, after seventh grade, pupils in orphanages who had already received some craft training (locksmith, metal worker, bookbinder, etc.) were sent straight to work in the factories or plants, where they were given a bed in a dormitory. They had to earn their own money for everything else. Something similar awaited me too, although I was completely unable to do such work, for I had not mastered any craft skills.

I had no idea exactly what would happen, but, although I was still a boy, I understood that I had to study further and finish at least high school.

THE FLIGHT

Otherwise, my life would be completely joyless.

I don't remember how, but I learned about some special 'military schools' that accepted students who had finished seventh grade with good or excellent grades. Graduates of these schools were sent to military colleges so that later they would become professional military men and commanders of the Red Army. There were several such schools in Moscow. Two or three Artillery schools and one Air Force school.

I had finished seventh grade with almost perfect scores and decided to apply to the Air Force school. The official name of the school was the First Moscow Specialty School of the Air Force. I immediately submitted all the documents, and when I arrived at the school on June 20th, the admissions committee informed me that I would be accepted if I passed another step called the mandate committee.

I was too young to understand what this meant. In response to my questioning him, the admissions officer lowered his voice and quietly explained to me that I would have to be evaluated for my political suitability to become a future military pilot and commander of the Red Army.

I instantly realized that I would hardly be recognized as suitable for this because of my father, who had been accused of treason against the state and had been killed during Stalin's purge of 1937. I feared I

THE FLIGHT

would never be able to go to this school because my father was considered a traitor.

Determined, and without hesitation, I asked when I would be able to pass the mandate committee. He handed me some paper in an envelope and pointed to a door at the end of the corridor, saying, "Go there."

I opened the door and entered, assuming I would end up in a reception area where I would have to wait for a long time, but I was wrong. I found myself in a large, bright office with a huge window. At a table near the window sat an officer. He raised his eyes, looked at me attentively, smiled, and said, "Hello, take a seat."

He pointed to a chair against the table, took my envelope, pulled out a piece of paper, and began to read it. I sat in silence and looked at him. He was a short stocky man of about thirty years of age with thick black curly hair and a typical face of someone from the Caucasus Mountain region; probably Armenian or Georgian, I thought.

Having finished reading, he raised his deep black eyes to me and asked, "Well, young man, do you want to study to become a military pilot?"

"I do," I replied.

He continued, "Where were you born?"

"In Moscow." I felt a bit anxious about the line of questioning.

THE FLIGHT

"And who are your parents?" His dark eyes glanced at me for a response.

I dreaded the question I knew was coming, "Mother is a nurse, currently unemployed."

"And your father?" He questioned.

There it was, I swallowed hard and answered, "I don't know, he hasn't lived with us for a long time."

This had the man's attention, "But where is he, what does he do?"

"I don't know," I lied out of caution.

He looked at me with raised eyebrows, "What do you mean, you don't know, has he completely abandoned you?"

"Yes, looks like he left us for good," a sickening feeling settled in the pit of my stomach.

The man pressed me, "But he's alive, he's not dead, is he?"

"I don't know, I think he's dead," I said as I exhaled quietly.

He stopped talking and looked at me carefully. "Tell the truth, was he repressed?" Repressed was a term they used for an enemy of the state, I knew what he was asking.

THE FLIGHT

"I think he was," I said, lowering my head to avoid looking him in the eye, "but he didn't live with us."

He fell silent again and appeared to be thinking. I sat silent too with my head down.

Finally, he said, "All right, ask your mother to come to me tomorrow at one o'clock. I'll talk to her." I said goodbye and walked out.

Back in the admissions office, I learned his name; Officer Martirosov. He alone comprised the extra mandate committee. It was up to him now whether I could finish high school or be deprived of this right.

The next day at one o'clock my mother and I were in Martirosov's office. He asked me to go out into the corridor, and he talked to her for about ten minutes. Then he opened the door and invited me to come in.

"I don't want to refuse you," he said, turning to me, "so I'll sign the permission form. Now, look here, Lev, study well." He smiled, shook my hand, and we left his office.

I looked at the clock hanging on the wall in the hallway. It was two o'clock in the afternoon on Saturday, June 21, 1941. My mom and I didn't know that there were just over twelve hours left before Nazi Germany would attack the Soviet Union before the cruelest war in history would start.

Nor did Officer Martirosov know, who, maybe simply

THE FLIGHT

because he was a decent man (or maybe for other reasons known only to him), allowed me to study at that time, to finish high school, and then, university. Ten years later, I clearly understood one more small detail in this story. With his signature, the senior political officer, most likely, also saved my life. If I had not been admitted into that special military Air Force school, in two years I would have been drafted into the infantry army, and once at the front, my chances of surviving there would have been minimal.

In the middle of October of 1941, the Nazis had come close to Moscow. My school (now the Surikov Institute), which was located on Lavrushensky Lane directly opposite the Tretyakov Art Gallery, received an evacuation order.

Around five hundred teachers and students lined up in a large column, to head to the train station. The command to march was given, and off we went. Suddenly someone shouted - "Leader, stop!" The entire column stopped - we stood for two or three minutes and started again.

It was evening and it was already dark by the time we had passed the Big Stone Bridge and began to turn to the right at St. Basil's Cathedral to Razina Street. A small German airplane appeared directly overhead, and we immediately dropped to the ground. The plane mistook us for a column of troops and dropped two bombs; one exploded on Razina Street in front of the column, the other at the end of the bridge behind us.

THE FLIGHT

These bombs were small, and no one was hurt. I think if we hadn't stood for those few minutes at the beginning of the journey, many of us would have been left lying on the pavement. We were exceptionally lucky.

Our school remained in evacuation in Siberia until the beginning of 1944 when I was already in my last year of high school. Despite our being safer than if we had stayed in Moscow, the food shortages due to the war still impacted us there. Food was rationed, and I was always hungry. A schoolmate of mine and I got to the point where we decided to take down the Soviet flag in the school cafeteria one night and give it to a woman in the local village in exchange for her feeding us lunch daily. She needed fabric, and we needed food. No one seemed to notice when we snuck out at lunchtime for the upgraded meal, soup.

In February of 1944, we returned to Moscow. At the end of May, our class finished high school, and all of us knew what was coming, we would join the military. The new mandate commission quickly determined who would go where. Most of the guys were sent to military flight schools. For presumably the same reason as my original mandate commission, I was sent with the minority of graduates to the school of military aviation mechanics in the city of Volsk, close to Saratov.

The question of whether I could succeed as a mechanic did not interest anyone. I was not

THE FLIGHT

mechanically inclined at all. I would never have been able to finish the schooling if not for the help of my friends and former classmates, who took turns doing all the work for me. They even performed my tasks for the final exams at the end of April 1945.

On May 8th, the war ended, and a week later our class went to Germany, where I joined the 283rd Aviation Fighter Division. There, as luck would have it, I was assigned to the division command and was given not a combat fighter, but a U-2 airplane. A single-engine low-speed biplane with two cabins and one low-power engine. It was used for communication and flights from regiment to regiment by the division command. It only needed refueling with gasoline and topping off engine oil periodically. Of course, I could do that, and I gradually learned the rest. There were three regiments in the division; they were scattered in a radius of 70-100 kilometers in the triangle of Halle-Leipzig-Dresden.

When any of my superiors took my airplane to the regiment, I usually sat in the second cabin, so I flew with them over central Germany for dozens of hours. I was only 18 years old. The senior officers of the division, veteran fighter pilots who had spent the war in the sky, carrying a dozen medals each, addressed me not as "Sergeant Perlov" but simply as "Lev."

They were extraordinary men, really the best men and the pride of Russia, who defended the Motherland and its people in that terrible war. They treated me

THE FLIGHT

like a son and taught and supported me. They did not give me any commands on duty but simply said, "Lev, please do this," and I was ready to fall over myself to please them. Or, as they say in Russian, to make myself into a pancake for them.

Almost sixty years have passed since that time, and they are probably no longer alive. But I can still see all of them in my mind, and as long as I live, I will cherish the brightest memory of them.

THE FLIGHT

THE FLIGHT

Lev, likely while stationed in Georgia
where he studied law remotely, circa 1948

THE FLIGHT

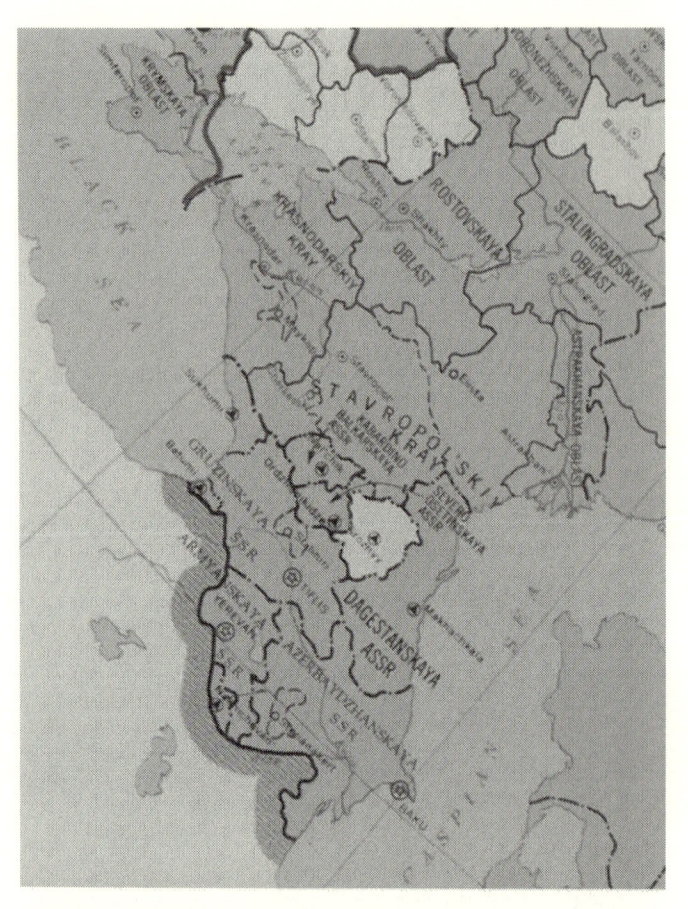

1960 Map of the Caucasus region with former Republic of Georgia (Gruzinskaya S.S.R.) and modern day Chechnya; Lev stationed here in the 1940's- 1950's

THE FLIGHT

Chapter Two

After the War

In February of 1946, our division was ordered to hand over all materials (i.e., planes) and relocate to Russia. We were transported in freight wagons with bunks and cast-iron stoves. Our destination was unknown to us. I remember after two weeks we reached the Volga River. In Saratov, we were taken to the city bathhouse. It was bitterly cold. We had no warm clothes except overcoats, and we were freezing.

From Saratov, our train went further down along the Volga. At the first stop of the day, someone jumped out of the wagon to see where we were going. Eventually, the train came to Transcaucasia but kept moving.

Finally, on the night of March 10th, the train stopped, but no one knew why. No commands were heard, so we kept sleeping. Early in the morning, we heard, "Unload!" The station sign read, Kobuleti.

Someone yelled, "I see the sea." We had arrived at the southernmost coast of the Black Sea in the Caucasus region in Georgia, at the best resort of Adjara, twenty-

THE FLIGHT

five kilometers from Batumi, where there was a long-dormant military airfield. The division headquarters and one of the regiments were located there. The division headquarters occupied a once luxurious, local hotel, which stood on the edge of the beach. The officers had taken rooms in private houses, and the mechanics of the control unit were lodged at the headquarters.

For two days after our arrival, the sun shone brightly. It was as warm as a summer's day, and the sea, which I was seeing for the first time, was splashing quietly at our feet. It felt like a dream, paradise.

Then a storm started; a frigid wind blew from the sea, and it rained for three weeks. We were all soaked to the skin, and there was nowhere to dry off. Paradise was lost; everyone was thinking only of alcohol.

This went on until mid-April when spring really arrived in Kobuleti. There were no airplanes, we had a nice life. In May 1946, the division received one U-2 airplane for connection purposes.

I was the only serviceman in the division, so this airplane was handed over to me. Everything went back to normal, only instead of Germany, we were flying over Georgia.

The division commander, an older Colonel, who had been through the whole war and had occasionally flown to regiments in Germany on my U-2, and

THE FLIGHT

sometimes on his fighter plane, could now fly only on the U-2. Our history together meant I often had free access to him, which even senior officers did not have.

It was then I realized I was wasting time in the army and decided to enroll in university. I wanted to enroll by correspondence into the Language, more specifically Philology, Department of Moscow University, and I knew that this would require a permission letter from the unit commander.

It wasn't long before I had to fly with the division commander to the regiment and, when we flew back, he had to wait for a car to take him back to headquarters. The airfield where my U-2 was based, located about five kilometers from Kobuleti, was just a field with a concrete strip, which served as a runway.

The commander rolled the plane to the edge of the airfield, and we got out of the cabins. He immediately sat down on the grass for a smoke break. The car coming for the commander would drop off a sentry to guard the airplane, but at that moment, it was only the two of us. I secured the plane in the parking lot and decided to talk to him about my intention to study.

"Comrade Colonel, may I address you on a personal matter?" I asked.

"Of course, Lev, sit down," he pointed to a place on the grass next to him. I sat down by his side and explained my intention, asking if it would be possible

THE FLIGHT

for me to get a permission letter from the command to study.

I did not know exactly who would sign such a letter, but I realized that such matters were not the function of the division commander. I also knew the relationship between him, and the Chief of Staff of the division was by no means friendly. The Chief of Staff was not a pilot, he was an unpleasant person, and he did not have the respect of the personnel. Everybody was simply afraid of him. That's the person from whom I was supposed to ask permission, but I knew he would say no.

"That's a good idea," said the commander, "but it will not be easy. Where do you want to enroll?"

I told him about my plans, mentioning that I would have to go to sessions twice a year. The Colonel thought for a while and said, "Lev, Moscow is far away and that is probably unrealistic. You should go to Tbilisi and find a university there. It is nearby, and while you are serving in the Caucasus, it will be easier to go there".

The Colonel continued, "Type up a letter and I'll sign it myself, then you can take it to the staff department and ask them to give you your high school diploma from your personal file.

I know the Chief of Staff will be against it, so if my signature alone doesn't work, come to my house

THE FLIGHT

tonight and tell me, and I'll sort it out later. In the meantime, don't say anything about it to anyone."

I did everything exactly as the Colonel instructed, and, although the Chief of Staff and a few others met my idea with hostility, in the end, the commander had the last word on the matter. After all, arguing with him, as they say in Russia, was like pissing against the wind - it lands on you anyway so it's not worth it.

Our commander was not only a kind and intelligent man, but he also knew the army well and understood the military bureaucracy. He was an old-school intellectual, an academic, who had been a university professor before the war, and he supported my efforts to get an education. Without his help, I doubt my education would have been allowed.

To my delight, in the fall of 1946, I became a student of the Tbilisi Branch of the All-Union Correspondence Law School. I studied there for three years.

At the end of 1949, the Tbilisi branch was closed, and all its management was imprisoned. They had been selling diplomas as bribes to anyone willing to pay. The case was investigated by officers from the Ministry of State Security in Moscow. Apart from mine, they found only one more personal file that contained a high school diploma. All the others had entered this Branch on a bribe.

I was transferred to the Moscow Branch, which I

THE FLIGHT

graduated from in December 1950 while still in the army. At that time, I was already serving in an air regiment, which was in Gudermes, in the Chechen region.

Fortunately, my next commander, a young Lieutenant Colonel, was from Moscow like me. This was great news for me, but I didn't have easy access to him like I had with my previous Colonel. I had already missed the in-person university session in the spring, and I could not miss another in-person session in Moscow. In desperation I asked his deputy, a Major, to help me.

The Major promised he would do his best, but he did even more than I could have hoped; he persuaded the commander to dismiss me immediately. The commander even asked me to take a letter to his parents living in Moscow.

I was extremely fortunate to have such great superiors; I remember thinking at the time that such amazing people could only be in the Air Force.

Ten days later, in Moscow, I took my first exam of my final year of school. In the following three weeks, I passed exams for all twelve subjects plus the state graduation exams, and I received my law degree.

I returned to the regiment in December, and in April of 1951, I was discharged from the army and finally returned to Moscow.

THE FLIGHT

Back in my hometown, things were difficult. I was a demobilized sergeant of the Soviet Army, who had been promised, by a governmental decree, to be supported by Soviet organizations and enterprises in matters of employment. I also had a higher legal education and was actively seeking employment; willing and able to take on any job.

However, beyond this, I was considered to be a cosmopolitan traitor, without roots in the Motherland of Russia, who had supposedly sold himself to international imperialism. Or, to put it simply, a Jew. No one anywhere would hire Jews.

Being Soviet citizens, we, Jews, were regarded as enemies of the people. If our so-called Greatest Leader Stalin hadn't died two years later, we would have been exterminated, although we didn't know that at the time. Because Jews, as a people group, had relatives outside the USSR, Stalin considered all of them potential traitors. At the time of his death, Stalin already had laid plans to expel all Jews from the European part of Russia to Siberia.

Thankfully, someone named Pavel helped me out. He was a relative of one of my army friends who had returned to Moscow with me, and he worked as a mechanic at one of Moscow's transport depots. The director of the depot was a Jew, and Pavel told him about me. So, thanks to them, in June of 1951, I got my first civilian position - dispatcher of the depot.

THE FLIGHT

But it was short-lived, because I was laid off to save the State money in December of that same year. Based on all of the truck route and expense records, there was actually plenty of work; our depot's trucks had cleared more snow in just two months, from November to December, than the amount of snow in a typical Moscow winter.

I ended up without work again, but not for long. A Jewish woman, an accountant at the transport depot, told her husband, Abram, about me. He was the head of the planning department at a small machine factory. It didn't take long before I was in his circle of friends. I was incredibly lucky again.

Abram was a brilliant economist and had recently worked as head of the economic planning department of a major aircraft factory. He was also the embodiment of wisdom and inexhaustible Jewish wit. If you spent any time around him, you were sure to be laughing uncontrollably at his comedic charm, as if you were enjoying a performance by Arkady Raikin, the famous Soviet comedian and performer.

Well past his fifties, Abram knew and understood the inner machinations of our Soviet reality. Very well-liked, connected, and admired by heads of government departments and ministries, Abram showed his disgust for the authorities and the "Great Leader," albeit diluted with obvious sarcasm to avoid getting in trouble.

THE FLIGHT

At the plant where Abram was working, the capital construction engineer had been seriously ill, apparently for a long time. So, Abram took me to the director and announced he had found a person to temporarily fulfill his duties.

Daniil, the director, was a very atypical Soviet chief. When others kicked out the Jews, he hired them, and he hired me as well, even though I confessed I did not know anything about construction.

"It's all right," he said, "you don't need to manage the construction, but you'll learn how to process documents; Abram will explain everything to you. Keep in mind, however, that there will be occasions when you'll have to do any job."

So, for the next three years, I worked for him as a construction engineer, a financier, a lawyer, a supply clerk, essentially as his right-hand man. Sometimes there was nothing to do for weeks, but I was still receiving my salary.

On March 5, 1953, our "Greatest Leader," Stalin, unexpectedly died of a stroke. It seemed like a miracle to me, but most Soviets were in mourning. They felt great grief at their loss and bewilderment at the future of the USSR. They had believed Stalin's propaganda, and the extent of his crimes was unknown at the time.

Thousands of people from all over Russia went to view his casket in the center of Moscow to pay their

THE FLIGHT

respects. I can remember exiting the metro station in the opposite direction that same day. Unlike the crowds, I was on the way to celebrate our miraculous deliverance from this awful dictator with my closest friends. Secretly, we toasted each other to the fact that the old dog croaked. Later, I found out there had been a stampede at Trubnaya Square because of the funeral, and many people had been crushed to death.

About a year and a half later, the engineer whom I was replacing had long since returned to work. Daniil invited me in, apologized, and said he couldn't keep me any longer.

I thanked him for his help in my time of need and expressed my sincere gratitude for everything I had learned from him. It was Daniil who taught me how to work and gave me practical knowledge and work experience. From him I learned a great life lesson about hard work - never accept the words "I can't" or "It's not possible," because he simply set a goal and demanded results, no matter how difficult they were to achieve.

Despite all that, no matter where I applied for another job, I was denied.

THE FLIGHT

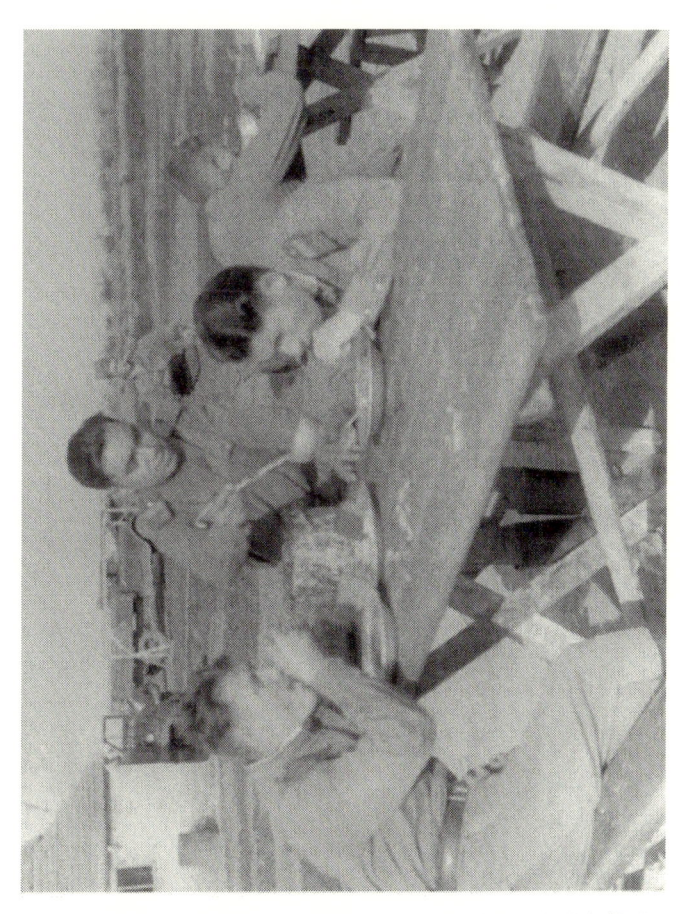

Lev (right) at military air base in Gudermes in modern day Chechnya, 30 miles east of Grozny, June 1950

THE FLIGHT

Faina, Lev's first wife, and Emma,
their dauther, circa 1964 outside of Moscow

THE FLIGHT

Chapter Three
Strapped for Cash

In the summer of 1954, I got married, and in March 1955, my first daughter, Emma, was born. The marriage was short-lived, and my hardships contributed to this. While I had an excellent relationship with her father, I felt my wife and her mother concluded I was unworthy and needed to be replaced. As soon as I realized this, I left, with much regret about leaving my child. By the spring of 1955, I started roaming the streets of Moscow like a hungry wolf, wondering where to get money for food.

One afternoon I was walking along the street called Kuznetsky Bridge. It was very crowded, and I came across a Jewish man who was holding a new edition of the *Decameron*, the Italian masterpiece by Bocaccio. Even though I knew I had no money to buy it, I asked him to show me the book out of curiosity.

After speaking for some time, the man asked me if I wanted to make some money. I replied, "Where have you been all my life?"

THE FLIGHT

It turned out his friend, Jan (pronounced Yan), was standing by in an entryway, hiding another fifty copies of the Decameron. Jan was a salesman at a bookstore in the center of Moscow, where the *Decameron* had arrived. This book was in high demand at the time. Jan had decided to take advantage of this opportunity and sell it on the street to make a profit and then reimburse the store for the original price. Within the next hour, the three of us quickly sold all of the books at a price five times higher than the nominal price.

The profit was divided between the three of us, and I left Kuznetsky Bridge with almost nine hundred rubles in my pocket (unthinkable money for me at the time) and arranged with Jan to meet at the same place the next morning.

For the next four months, we continued our scheme, and I no longer needed money.

Jan was a surprisingly good businessman, but, because of his excessive greed, he was not always an honest partner. I remember once saying to him, "Jan, your greed can ruin you."

I don't know whether he recalled my warning when, six years later, he found himself in prison. I think, because of his greed, he foolishly traded currency under the very nose of the KGB. Yes, Jan Rokotov, my acquaintance, became a famous currency dealer.

In September or October of 1955, the Soviet government issued a decree criminalizing minor ventures directly targeting businessmen like us. Obviously, I had to immediately give up my business and somehow find a job.

I wasted no time, and although I successfully sold books, mostly on weekends, I continued to look for a job.

In contrast, Jan was eventually caught exchanging rubles for foreign currency, which was illegal and considered immoral by Leninist ideology. In 1961, he was tried by the Russian Republic Supreme Court and charged with the death penalty at the age of 33 years. His death sent shock waves throughout the country.

In the evenings I took courses designed for construction estimators. In the fall of 1955, I finished with excellent marks and received a state certificate. Considering my previous three-year experience with Daniil, by that time, I had become quite a qualified construction estimator.

Estimators were needed in many places, but I was usually either turned down or offered a laughable salary to turn down on my own. One anti-Semite,

THE FLIGHT

smirking cheekily, offered me five hundred rubles a month. I could barely restrain myself from spitting in his face. This was long before Khrushchev's monetary reform at the end of 1960, which meant, according to the new money, it was fifty rubles. By comparison, a janitor at the factory where I worked the previous year received seven hundred rubles for working part-time.

I felt cornered and had to do something drastic to obtain my "Right to Labor" which was guaranteed by the Stalinist Constitution.

Entering the lobby of the All-Union Communist Party on Old Square, found the telephone number of the Construction Department of the Moscow State Committee, went into a telephone booth, and dialed that number.

"Instructor Kydryashov of the Construction Department," I heard as the phone was answered.

"Comrade Kydryashov, this is (I respectfully gave my surname, first name, patronymic, year of birth, and nationality) speaking to you. I am the son of a posthumously exonerated Communist from Moscow, I have a specialty as a construction estimator, but no one will hire me." I was sure my explanation would be sufficient. "Please order me a pass so I can come and explain my situation to you."

THE FLIGHT

Without hesitation, he replied, "Comrade Perlov, I can't order you a pass."

"Why would that be, I wonder? Are you afraid of me? I can assure you that I don't have a gun, but if I did, I'd probably have shot a couple of anti-Semites by now." I must admit I got carried away.

I continued in the same vein, saying improper things in a raised voice, until I noticed that a caveman in a policeman's uniform had approached my booth. I had opened it so as not to suffocate. He stood about three meters away, looking at me directly, but I didn't care.

Gratefully, the man on the phone, obviously realizing he was dealing with a desperate man, asked me to calm down and to tell him everything in detail over the phone. So, I did.

"But what does the Party Moscow Committee have to do with it?" he asked me rhetorically upon completion of my detailed story, "We are not engaged in employment."

Exasperated, I responded, "Comrade, "I don't think you understand me. I have used up all the means available to me to get a job, and I believe sincerely in our Constitution, which guarantees me the right to work."

THE FLIGHT

In desperation I continued, "In order to prevent starvation, I currently earn my livelihood by selling books on the Kuznetsky Bridge. If I am arrested and prosecuted for minor speculation under the new decree, I will demand you be summoned to court as an authoritative witness representative of the Soviet authorities who refused to help me exercise my constitutional right to labor, despite my urgent request for such help. I think this will mitigate my faults. If the court refuses to do so, I will declare a hunger strike."

Knowing I also had a law degree, my last tirade made an impression on him. Judging by his voice, he was still a young, not quite hardened party bureaucrat. After a short hesitation, he said, "All right, go for a walk and call me in a couple of hours."

I supposed he intended to run the matter by his superiors, and when I called him again, he said, "Go to the personnel department of Glavmosstroy and ask for the chief. I have already called her, and she promised to help you."

Half an hour later I was let into the chief's office. One glance at her was enough for me to suspect I would be dealing with a full-blown anti-Semite, but I introduced myself. "I'm Lev Eduardovich Perlov. You got a call

THE FLIGHT

from the Construction Department of the Moscow State Party Committee regarding me."

"Yes, yes," her reply was dismissive, "Take the form from my secretary, fill it out, and come back in a week."

This was a delay tactic I was very familiar with. Instead, I took the completed form out of the side pocket of my jacket and handed it to her.

"Ah, so you're a lawyer," she said in a feignedly disappointed tone as she glanced at the questionnaire.

"I am also a construction estimator, and I would be most grateful if you could reasonably explain to me how a law degree, as well as any other higher education, would prevent me from being employed in that field?" It was probably not in my best interest, but the question deliberately sounded confrontational.

"No, no, we don't need lawyers," she said.

"We shall see," I replied. I took my questionnaire back and walked out.

I called the instructor at the construction department from the lobby downstairs and, after telling him how I had been received, said something to the effect that it

THE FLIGHT

was not wise to use me, in my desperate situation, as a soccer ball.

I realized this made him feel uncomfortable as he said, "Wait ten minutes and go up to her again." I waited and went up again.

The secretary told me the chief was "out" but handed me a signed referral to work in Glavmosstroy's Construction Trust Number 17, telling me to call if I had any difficulties there.

My first encounter with the personnel department of the Trust didn't go as smoothly as I had hoped but eventually, they handed me a signed referral to work as an estimator in one of the construction departments of this Trust.

When I first arrived at the job location an hour later, I saw a young woman sitting on the steps. When I got to the porch, she asked, "Are you Perlov?"

"Yes," I said, guessing it was the construction department's personnel officer, who had already been alerted and was waiting for me outside.

"Welcome," she said, "Give me your referral, and I'll register you right away. Come on, I'll introduce you to the staff of the technical department." She was a Party organizer in the construction department. Everyone

THE FLIGHT

just called her Tonya.

I remember once, Tonya gave us nonparty employees a copy of the "secret" report of Khrushchev at the 20th Party Congress on Stalin's crimes. Upon reading it, horrified and traumatized, I had a momentary explosion of indignation. I grabbed the gilded framed portrait of the mustachioed despot off the technical department wall and threw it on the floor.

When Tonya returned, seeing the portrait was missing she asked with panic in her voice, "Where's the portrait?" When I explained I had taken it down she insisted I return it to the wall. "Please hang it back up or I'll be punished."

Having gotten to know Tonya better, I was relieved to learn she had little in common with typical Soviet personnel officers of that period. I couldn't let her get into trouble over a missing portrait. There was nothing to do but put the tyrant back on the wall.

At that time, in 1956, under pressure from the World Labor Organization, Khrushchev repealed a law that denied the Soviet worker the right to resign at will and consolidated this right into a new law. Workers could now resign at will. The authorities, however, did not officially announce this, and, except for lawyers and personnel department workers, very few people knew about it at the time.

I worked in the construction department for a year with Tonya, where I learned a lot of new things as a professional. In October of 1956, I agreed to move to a better-paid job in a prestigious institute.

When I submitted a letter of resignation, the new head of the construction department, who had recently appeared in our organization, was outraged by this impudence and refused to accept or sign it. Tonya and I tried in vain to explain to him those things had changed, and he was violating the new law.

I called the Regional Prosecutor's office, asked for the general supervision prosecutor on the phone, and made a verbal complaint against my chief. The next morning at work, I found my resignation letter with his signature on my desk. A week later, I started my new job.

From October 1956 to December 1961, I worked as an estimator on a thermoelectric project, "Teploelektroproekt", and then on a hydro project, "Gidroproekt", participating in major residential and industrial construction projects. I was constantly learning from more experienced estimators. During those years, I became an experienced estimating professional, but then I had a new problem. My

THE FLIGHT

superiors often wanted me to work for my less experienced colleagues who often earned more. Sometimes it became a serious conflict, but I always knew how to stand up for myself, and I had long stopped being afraid.

In 1957, as luck would have it, my half-sister Louisa from my father's second marriage was hired. I realized it was her, but she did not say a word to me. I figured she probably didn't recognize me, as she had been very young when I left for Siberia with the military school. I had stopped by her house once when I first returned to Moscow, but her grandmother had kicked me out, thinking their problems had come from my father being accused of being an enemy of the state. I did not know what to do; perhaps she too was simply avoiding me.

Finally, one day, after I stepped into the hall, Louisa came out after me and yelled, "Levka!!!"

I responded, "Now you get it!? I was not sure if you were avoiding me!"

She had just been given a list of everyone in our office, and she saw my name. I was reunited with my sisters.

THE FLIGHT

THE FLIGHT

Louisa, Lev's half-sister,
circa 1955, Moscow

THE FLIGHT

Lora, Lev's second half-sister, circa 1960, Moscow

THE FLIGHT

Chapter Four

Unexpected Romance

By the beginning of the sixties, Soviet citizens had gradually weaned themselves from the cruel clutches of the Stalinist regime, which had constantly and mercilessly crushed them in the thirties, forties, and early fifties.

After Stalin passed away, there had been a struggle for power among the heirs of the half-crazed dictator, like crabs climbing over each other in a pot of boiling water. That struggle also ended.

It was now Khrushchev who reigned on the Soviet throne. I liked to call him the great "pig farmer" because of his previous experience in agriculture. He was barely literate, fussy, and talkative, but, compared to Stalin, not a threat to life (unless you count Jan Rokotov and his associates, whom he had executed). Nevertheless, the living standards of the people remained low.

In Moscow, where I found myself, the housing problem was most acute. Entire families occupied just one room in a "communal" apartment, meaning an apartment with a shared kitchen, whereas other

THE FLIGHT

families also lived in only one room. I was living, if one could call it that, in an 11' x 11' room, with my mentally ill mother, in an apartment with an outhouse and no running water, where two other families also lived. I used to brush my teeth, wash my face, and shave with my electric razor when I got to work in the morning.

I would come home late in the evening only to sleep. I would leave early in the morning to go to work, and on the weekends, I simply went somewhere outdoors. I would mostly spend my time after work, as well as on Saturdays and Sundays, in two large Moscow libraries - the Lenin Library or the Historical Library. I would often go there as soon as they opened and stay until they closed.

Once when I became extremely ill with severe flu, out of necessity, I asked the doctor to put me in the hospital and I stayed there for ten days.

Weekly I went to the Sandunov (public) baths to wash up. They had laundry there, so I would leave my dirty underwear to be cleaned. The next week I would exchange my other pair for the clean pair, and in this way, I had one pair of clean underwear for each week.

I ate in canteens and eateries, mostly in those at work and in the libraries, but in many others as well, as I wandered around the city. In short, it was the life of a vagabond-bum, but I was neither morally nor physically depressed, for I was still young (34 years

THE FLIGHT

old), healthy, independent, well-educated, had enviable energy, and a keen interest in women.

I worked, earning a minimal income to support myself, and I gave part of my salary to my mother. However, I did not want to live like that forever. In the spring of 1961, I started a desperate struggle with the Soviet authorities for a proper place to live.

I wrote applications to the district housing department at my place of residence, referring to the new laws relating to assistance for families of exonerated Communists such as my father, and I constantly shoved the certificate, from the military prosecutor's office regarding my father's exoneration, into the bureaucrats' faces.

After repeated refusals, I filed various complaints with the district executive committee, at all levels. Their answers, often quite verbose, in general, boiled down to one point; Dear Comrade, Get Lost! Life went on.

One nice summer evening, I headed to the Lenin Library after work. I approached a row of phone booths to the left of the entrance to Revolution Square metro station. It was a well-known date spot and there were always a lot of people there; some were making phone calls, others were just standing and waiting.

I glanced at the crowd and immediately noticed a young, attractive, slender woman who was obviously

THE FLIGHT

waiting for someone. I wanted to approach her right away but decided to wait a little longer. Five minutes passed, and no one came up to her. As always in such cases, I jokingly spurred myself on, "Well, Lev, it is time to make a move, Mother Russia demands it," and quickly approached.

"Young lady, I beg your pardon, but I am sure that the man you are waiting for has had the impudence of not showing up today," I bravely started the conversation.

"No, he'll be here soon, " she replied.

Smiling, I persisted, "I admire your optimism, but I bet it's not justified."

Amused, she smiled back, "I can see you're a pessimist."

We chatted for another ten minutes, and it became obvious that he was not going to show up. I invited her to go to Manezhnaya Square, where there was an exhibition. I don't remember what kind of exhibition it was, but I know that it had something to do with the English language.

I had developed a passion for the language, to satisfy my intellectual hunger, and I had a premonition it would be useful in the future. But the main reason, of course, was I wanted to show off to my date Valentina, and hoped my knowledge of the language of Shakespeare and Byron would be sufficient to do so.

THE FLIGHT

When I approached one of the stands at the Manezhnaya, I started reading something in English and began to translate, but one word was unfamiliar to me (the text was difficult) and I stumbled.

Valentina immediately told me its meaning and continued reading. Her pronunciation was flawless; she sounded just like one of the BBC's female newscasters, which I tried to listen to when I visited a friend who owned a high-quality radio.

She spoke to me in perfect English, and my esteem for her rose immediately. I was a self-taught learner, and so far, I was only able to read English, so I was embarrassed and delighted at the same time.

I learned she had graduated from the Moscow Pedagogical University in the English department and was now working in one of the "mailboxes" (a term used for a top-secret, military agency that used a mail code as a classified location) as a translator of technical texts. It was obvious to me that she was completely unfamiliar with technology, so this use of her English surprised me somewhat, and I told her so. She smiled sadly in response, and I didn't inquire further. I liked her more and more.

We walked around Alexandrovsky Garden for a while, a park just outside the Kremlin, and then I offered to take her home. She assured me she lived not far from the Sokol metro station and thought it would be best for us to part in Revolution Square.

THE FLIGHT

I asked her to give me her phone number, but she explained she didn't have a phone at home and that it was not advisable to call her at work. I could do nothing more, but she gave me her word that we would see each other again and agreed to come to the same place for another date in two days.

When I got back home, quite unexpectedly, I received a notice from the district executive committee that the following day I could meet with the Deputy Chairman for Housing Issues, i.e., the main person in charge of housing in our district.

When the appointed hour came (I remember it was toward evening), I sat in the Deputy Chairman's waiting room. He was away; apparently running late. Finally, when the working day was over, he appeared accompanied by two or three people.

The secretary reminded him that I was waiting for an appointment. He came up to me, introduced himself, gave me a handshake, and apologized for being late, saying that he had been busy all day and that he was very tired. I could see that for myself, he did not look well, and, strange as it was given my position of having waited so long to get help with my housing, I felt involuntary sympathy for him.

I was somehow soothed by his intelligence and his calm, sincere politeness, and respect, which made him so different from all the civilian Party and Soviet functionaries with whom I had dealt so far. I

THE FLIGHT

immediately told him that I could come another day. He thanked me, we said goodbye, and I left, forgetting to ask the secretary to schedule another appointment for me.

The following evening, after my failed appointment with the Deputy Chairman for Housing Issues, I went to wait for Valentina and stood at the vending machines at the same subway station where I had left her two days prior. I kept staring fixedly at the exit door of the station so as not to miss her, and she appeared 5 minutes later. I took her for a walk in Alexandrovsky Garden again.

I had no money to invite her to coffee at "Cafe Moscow" or to "The National" restaurant, and I was of course embarrassed about that, but I did not give the appearance of being so. She acted naturally, in no way indicating that she expected such an invitation.

It was a beautiful June evening. We sat down on an out-of-the-way bench and learned more about each other. Her situation was not as favorable as I had assumed.

Valentina had come to Moscow from the provinces to study, and she had graduated from university. She had no Moscow registration and was living with a friend, trying to remain invisible to the authorities. Registration in Moscow was required to live and work in the city.

THE FLIGHT

I realized she would understand, so I told her how I was living, about my attempts to get decent housing, and about yesterday's failed appointment at the district executive committee. In passing I casually mentioned the name of the person who would decide if I would finally get my living space.

"So, you live in the Timiryazevsky district?" Valentina asked me.

I was surprised she knew what district I was living in, "Yes, and how do you know?"

"I know the man who had to reschedule on you," she replied, "it's not for public knowledge, of course, but I think I can trust you; he's my relative. He helped me get a job after university without residence registration. That's why he can't help me with housing, he doesn't have the power to do so."

"Valechka," I immediately blurted out, "God sent us to each other. Help me get my own room, we'll get married, and I'll provide you with registration at my place. You won't have any more problems."

"My God," she said, "you don't know me at all, and I don't know you. I'm just dumbfounded by your offer, and I don't know what to say." There was no need for me to respond.

We could not have known the events which would open up for us following our conversation.

THE FLIGHT

As fate would have it, a couple of days later, a friend of mine at work recommended me as an honorable person to her aunt. Her aunt needed someone to look after her private apartment for a few months. By the end of the week, I had moved in, as I essentially owned nothing but the clothes on my back.

Valentina and I were people of similar fates in an absurd and cruel world, but we used my temporary living situation to get intimate quickly, brighten our lives, and learn almost everything about each other.

We were both young, had received an excellent education, had some work that did not correspond to our education or abilities, and had no roof over our heads. We had nothing, not even the necessities of life.

She shared with me that in the spring of '59, before final exams at university, she had been invited to the local Communist Party Office for an interview. The "interviewer" turned out to be a KGB captain, who was trying to recruit her as a "swallow" to seduce foreigners in Moscow, so they could extort and recruit them to cooperate with the KGB.

He insisted it was her patriotic duty and promised her the best conditions: permanent residence in the capital, the rank of KGB officer, high pay for "work", a private apartment in the center of Moscow, a two-month vacation every year in a special health resort by the seaside in the South, and so on.

THE FLIGHT

The captain made it clear to her that refusal of such an offer, for any reason other than marriage, would be interpreted as a spiteful act towards the all-powerful agency and hinted at the consequences. He discouraged her from getting married as well.

"I almost threw up right on the paper he wanted me to sign," she said, "but I held back and asked for time to think, so he gave me a month." What was she to do?

At the time some guy was looking after her and she quickly agreed to marry him. She wrote to the KGB officer, explaining that, while she was flattered by his proposal, she was pregnant and could not accept his offer.

As might be expected, the marriage was ill-fated. She gave birth to a baby girl but left her husband and filed for divorce within six months. The child was taken in by his parents, who lived far from Moscow, and Valentina only saw her twice after that. Of course, she missed her child.

During my temporary housing, Valentina and I were both focused on the same goal, getting my own place. She helped me with this, and we lived in the new place amicably for a year and a half. We married, and she became a legal Moscow resident.

Unfortunately, we parted in the summer of 1963. She was a very worthy woman, but she was naturally

THE FLIGHT

drawn to her child and the problem constantly weighed on our relationship. I knew if the child came to live with us, I would have to tolerate her father's presence in our life, which was unacceptable to me, especially in the conditions of our miserable Soviet existence. I simply could not put myself and my family in any kind of dependence on a stranger.

In addition, I knew that if we were ever allowed to leave, the authorities would not need a better excuse to "extend our stay" in the U.S.S.R.

I was left alone living as a bachelor, but this time I had a room. It was in a two-story, two-family brick house, which had become a communal apartment where four other people lived, each in their own rooms. There was a woman in her forties who pretended to be younger, an elderly couple who occupied two rooms, and a woman in her sixties.

The apartment was on two levels: the rooms of the young woman, the old man, and mine were upstairs; the other two rooms, the toilet room, and the kitchen, were downstairs. There was no hot water and no full bathroom; so, I kept going to the Sandunov baths.

Tensions between tenants were a common occurrence, usually over trivial things, and life in that communal apartment was indescribably nasty. But millions of "happy Soviet people" lived even worse than my neighbors and me.

THE FLIGHT

Soon the old man's wife died. She had been a quiet, harmless old woman. I don't think he needed a new wife, but he was, understandably, afraid of having the second room taken away from him. So, he immediately married some distant relative or acquaintance of his and registered her there.

This old woman turned out to be the opposite of his first wife. She ordered her new husband, and two other neighbors around and loudly and insolently claimed her unquestionable superiority in every apartment squabble.

Since I almost always left home early in the morning, came home in the evening, and spent most of my time in my room, I was not affected too much by her antics.

THE FLIGHT

Lev, 1958, Moscow

THE FLIGHT

Rosa in the hat Lev noticed upon their first encounter,
Moscow, Circa 1967

THE FLIGHT

Chapter Five
Finding My Calling

When I finally got my own room in December of 1961, I was working at the Organization for Engineering and Research of Hydro-Electric Power, located across the city. That required me to take three kinds of transportation to get to work, which was not ideal.

Two months later I moved to another leading design and research institute, the Central Research and Design Institute of Housing (CRDIH), which was a ten to fifteen-minute walk from my home.

The apartment building where I lived was on the edge of a magnificent old oak park, which was aptly named Dubki (Oaks) Park. On the other side of the park was my new job location. At that time, the area was a barely populated, quiet suburb of Moscow. Walking past the tall perennial oaks in the morning and listening to the birds singing, I enjoyed the nature and solitude.

I did not have a great singing voice, so I would recite to myself the lyrics of Lermontov's famous poem, *I Come Out To The Path Alone*:

THE FLIGHT

"So that the enchanting voice would ready

day and night sing to me of love,

And the oak, evergreen and shady,

would decline toward me and rustle above."

These minutes of my day were like a fairy tale, like shots from the movie *"The Great Waltz,"* the 1938 Academy Award-winning movie about the life of Johann Strauss II.

Because of all I had been through and the lack of any reward for hard work under communism, there was no incentive to be loyal to either the Soviet regime or to any of the regime's employers. Everyone was treated the same. So, when choosing a job, like most employees, I thought only of my interests. This new place of work suited me better than all the previous ones for a number of reasons. I worked there for twelve years.

In 1965, I was promoted to the position of patent reviewer at my job. Using my legal education and my knowledge of construction techniques and technology, I excelled in the role.

I dare even say that I gained the respect of accomplished engineers and scientists, and at the same time, the dislike of those scientists and engineers who were less successful in their field and served primarily as administrators.

THE FLIGHT

Many of these administrators wanted a Soviet patent in their name to improve their dissertation or their upward mobility, and they constantly bombarded me with their ideas. As a rule, these ideas were not remarkable for their technical novelty and did not satisfy the main requirement for a patent.

In response to my refusal to file a patent application for them, some of the authors were dissatisfied and simply tried to pressure me. Needless to say, this did not work. Regardless of the official position of the person making demands, my resistance, as always, grew in direct proportion to their pressure. My legal knowledge gave me a definite advantage over them.

As a patent specialist, I had wasted no time familiarizing myself with technical solutions in industrial housing construction patents and had a good understanding of which ideas were patentable, and which were not. I tried in vain to explain this to them.

Of course, I did not care much about their upward mobility, and I refused to cooperate, so their dislike for me gradually increased.

On the other hand, at the personal level, my life took a fortunate turn. In the late spring of 1967, I was leaving a meat and produce shop when in walked an extremely attractive young woman in what appeared to be a white fur hat.

THE FLIGHT

"Young woman, is that a fur hat or your actual hair?" I asked curiously.

"A hat," she replied as she proceeded into the store, "I am so sick and tired of you all," she muttered under her breath, obviously annoyed by my comment.

She and her mother had stopped in to buy sausages, but there was a lengthy line to pay for them. Her mom told her, "Why don't you head home and start peeling potatoes for dinner?"

Meanwhile, I had been waiting at the door for her to exit. As she was leaving, I inquired, "Young lady, are you busy tonight?"

"No, I am not," she responded to my surprise.

Encouraged, I asked, "Would you like to go to the movies with me?"

"Sure," she replied.

"Ok let's meet at the movie theatre at 8," I smiled, quite pleased with myself.

She smiled back, "See you there."

I was there waiting at 8 pm sharp. She was very prompt, which impressed me.

THE FLIGHT

After the movie ended and we had walked outside, I asked her where she lived. It turned out she lived two trolley stops from the theatre. I lived two trolley stops from the theatre in the opposite direction, so I decided to walk her all the way home. It was a 20-minute walk, and I entertained her by reciting Russian poetry to her.

I felt certain at that point that she understood I was a walking encyclopedia. I could answer all her questions because I had spent so much time in the libraries and had memorized a lot of literature and history.

For some reason I thought it would impress her, so I boasted, "My last name only has six letters!"

She responded, "*My* last name only has *six* letters!"

Astounded I asked, "Oh are you Jewish?"

"No, my grandfather was a Swede," she explained.

I like this woman; I thought to myself.

I started dating her regularly, and we got married in December 1967. There were no religious institutions allowed at that time in the U.S.S.R., so, like everyone else, we got married simply by signing the appropriate documents at the civil registry office. Our two best friends accompanied us as witnesses.

In the summer of 1969, the American astronauts

THE FLIGHT

landed on the moon, and everyone was talking about it. One day I walked into one of the rooms of the scientific department of the Institute. There were about twenty employees who were animatedly discussing the success of the USA. I knew all of them, and they all knew me.

One of them turned to me and said, "Lev, please comment on the American moon landing."

I took the pose of a wise prophet and said wryly, "I still think that the first man on the Moon will be a Soviet man." I was mocking Soviet propaganda, which often boasted incredulous claims that could never be true.

I don't know if it was a reaction to my comment, but a couple of weeks later I was informed by the Institute's management that our patent-licensing group, which I headed (two other female patent scientists worked with me), was being reorganized into a patent-licensing department of four people. Everyone was puzzled by the change.

They invited a patent specialist from the neighboring Institute of Public Buildings to head the department. I knew this "colleague" well. He and I had been on a first-name basis for a long time.

He often came to me for professional advice, knowing nothing about patent matters. He was an absolute and utter numskull. Anytime I tried to explain something to him, he just looked at me in confusion. I would sigh

THE FLIGHT

with relief when he pretended to understand my counsel and finally left.

Soon this guy was "in charge" of us. I tried not to show my attitude toward him; however, I was incapable of hypocrisy.

On the first day, he looked at me and asked, "Well, where should we start?"

"Are you asking me?" I asked, "Ask yourself, you're the boss after all," I replied. Both women lowered their eyes. There was a long silence.

I was sitting in a chair in the corner of a room where a lot of space was taken up by closets, and there was no room for a fourth desk. He remained silent. After about five minutes I said, "I'm going to the library to take a look at the patent literature. If you need me, call there, I don't have a place to work here."

I went down to the reading room of the library, where I had a desk. The head of the library was a friend of mine, so she let me work there, and even study English grammar when I had time.

For the following two weeks, we played the same game. Then the Principal Director of Scientific Research, who knew me well, called me in. He asked me what was going on in the patent department, and I informed him that I had been waiting for guidance for a long time.

THE FLIGHT

Exasperated, he begged me to be more cooperative.

A couple of days later, the head of the Institute's Technical Information Department, with whom I was on excellent terms, came to the library; we addressed each other simply by name. He was a front-line soldier and an intellectual who spent every spare minute studying Japanese. He was well aware of my similar obsession with English.

Smiling broadly, he told me that he had been authorized by the administration to ask if I would agree to be transferred to his department to do technical translations from English. He did not have to convince me for a minute. I became a translator, and that was the last time I changed my profession.

My relationship with my new boss, Volodya, was excellent. His translation department consisted of women and recent graduates of the Institute of Foreign Languages. They had no experience with technical texts on construction in either language.

Volodya gave me the most difficult texts, including American and British patents, and for this, I persuaded him to let me work at home to increase my productivity. He was setting deadlines for me, and the rest, as he said, was "none of his business". That's what I needed. I started coming to the Institute only twice a week to drop off completed translations and pick up new ones.

THE FLIGHT

After a month or so, I became so proficient at it that I could finish my daily assignment by noon. But of course, I modestly kept quiet about that. English was my job and my hobby. I couldn't think of anything better for myself.

After lunch, I went to the Red Square almost every day, where I got acquainted with American and British tourists and practiced my spoken English. Not that my boss wanted to, but it was impossible to call me at home to check what I was doing. I simply didn't have a phone at my place.

Everyone was very satisfied - the translation customers, the translator himself, and his boss.

I did have to be careful speaking to Westerners, as the authorities forbade it. However, because my English was self-taught, I needed this to hone my skills and perfect my craft. Importantly, through these conversations, I learned that the information the Soviet regime was giving us, namely that life in the West was worse than life in the USSR, was false.

The more I thought about it, the change in my career to become an English translator felt like a trout being set free in a river heading toward the ocean. The new career had set things in motion, and I was the one, like that trout, who would have to decide in which ocean I would swim. In that regard, it became increasingly clear over time what my main prospect was.

THE FLIGHT

THE FLIGHT

Rosa, pregnant with Katia at the dacha outside of Moscow, Krasnaya Pahra, 1972

THE FLIGHT

Lev and Katya (5 months old), June 1973,
two months before emigrating

THE FLIGHT

Chapter Six
Closer to Freedom

By the spring of 1973, my wife, Rosa, who is Russian Orthodox, and I had two precious children: four-and-a-half-year-old Sofia and four-month-old Katya. That same year, Rosa and I spent a lot of time discussing our future and the future of our children. We were concerned about staying in the Soviet Union, especially for their sake, but emigration was not allowed.

As a result of persistent anti-Semitism, Jews' experience in the USSR continued to be much more painful compared to other nationalities. Israel's victory in the Middle East in the "June War" of 1967 served as a wake-up bugle for Jewish dignity. The most courageous soon raised their voices and demanded the right to emigrate. The call of fearlessness had a snowball effect on us all. Thousands of Moscow Jews, most of them intellectuals, soon realized that the moment was coming when they would have to make the hard choice - stay put or request permission to leave.

THE FLIGHT

All of them knew that, at a minimum, such a request would mean friction with Soviet power, which was pervasive. Sometimes, it also meant more dire consequences: loss of employment, and/or decent housing, deprivation of scientific and social honors, including travel abroad, and even prison. Meanwhile, the number of exit visas grew grudgingly slowly.

However, the West, particularly the United States, soon made its demand for free Jewish emigration well-known to the Kremlin. The late Senator Henry Jackson (God rest his soul) decisively used his enormous influence to spearhead this effort in Washington, the rest of the US, and before world public opinion. That helped a lot; the outflow of Jews gradually began to mount. Rosa pointed out to me that this could be our opportunity to emigrate for our children's sake. But we could not get to Israel without a sponsor, typically a relative, who would send a formal invitation. It was during that time that I ordered and received, through the network of Jewish activists in Moscow, an invitation from the family of my fictitious Aunt, to join them in Israel.

At that time, Rosa worked as a music teacher in a Moscow elementary school. She played the piano and sang well, especially arias from operas and romantic songs. She even tried to teach me to sing, however, she said that a bear had stepped on my ear, a Russian expression meaning I was tone-deaf. In the end, she somehow managed to teach me one folk song called, "You and I Are Two Banks Along One River."

Our educational and employment achievements, even our existence itself, seemed to be of no importance to our mighty Socialist State. We had never challenged the authorities, nor could we possibly have been in possession of any military secrets, all we wanted to do was bid farewell to the state. With the current situation in Jewish emigration, we had not anticipated the State might have any objection to our departure. In March of 1973, I went to the Moscow Visa Office and picked up an application form for the exit visas for my family.

At that time, my mother was seventy-two, still mentally unstable but otherwise in sound health. She lived alone in a small apartment not far from ours and was quite able to take daily care of herself. I helped her financially on a regular basis because her state pension was negligible. But no matter how hard I tried, maintaining a normal family relationship had been difficult. I visited her and carefully mentioned the possibility that we might soon leave the country. I also suggested that she consider joining us. As I expected, she refused. "No," she said, "I am not going

THE FLIGHT

anywhere..." I tried to convince her to at least think the matter over, telling her that she should not stay behind all alone. I tried in vain.

The next several weeks were spent in appeals to reason and mercy. Rosa came along carrying little Katya in her arms and cried for hours begging my mother to join us or at least to sign a paper required by the Visa Office of all emigrants from their parents. No, she said repeatedly, she'd never get involved in this and never sign anything, "You can do whatever you want, just leave me alone." Finally, I came to realize that the terrible legacy of the past would never let her be at peace with herself or with the world around her. All those days, talking to my mother, I often froze from a sinister sensation that a black, hairy hand stretched out of Stalin's grave about to grab and strangle my little family, one by one.

Without the papers which we begged my mother to sign, the Visa Office would not accept my application. At that time, any Jew who wished to receive an exit visa to leave the country for good had to submit that document from his parents. It did not matter whether the applicant was a teenager or a senior citizen, and whether the parents were in their 20s or 90s. The parents, or one of them, if still alive, had to express to the authorities their opinion about their child's desire

THE FLIGHT

to emigrate to Israel. They could give consent, or simply write *no objections*, or they could object either mildly or vigorously. Whatever they wished! But the paper had to be attached to your application. Without it, the Visa Office (staffed mostly with KGB females on detail) would throw your papers back at you.

Not that the document played any role when one's application was considered. The Soviets knew perfectly well how ridiculous this requirement was, even in terms of their own law; but the parent's signature on the paper had to be certified by the emigre's local housing office, and the Police State had a strong interest in exposing the "traitor's" family to its neighbors. A *character paper*, which was required from the applicant's employer, served the same purpose as his or her coworkers.

As for the *character paper*, I was just lucky. I had an excellent business rapport with a senior researcher at the Institute (Vadim was his first name). He was a moderately active Communist party member, who had recently, and quite suddenly been chosen and elected by the district party committee to lead our institute's Communist party organization. The symbolic election, a formal communist ritual, soon followed.

THE FLIGHT

Vadim really was one of the guys at work, and, although the guys were puzzled by his meteoric rise to power, at the same time, they welcomed the fact. In our scientific world replete with mediocre careerists and KGB informants, he had a reputation for being a decent, honest, and straightforward man.

Vadim was also a real scientist and an effective manager. Everyone liked and respected him. It was Vadim who chaired the institute's party bureau meeting where my *character papers,* required by the Visa Office, were discussed in my presence. This had to be done in accordance with the established procedures, although it never even occurred to me to join the party. I do not know who drafted the paper, but Vadim's was to be the most important signature on that document. He was the top local party boss, and he had the last word.

The meeting secretary read the proposed text; I prepared myself for the worst and was surprised by its moderate tone. It even praised my performance on the job and contained no *rightly deserved condemnation* of my decision to abandon my Socialist homeland. None. It seemed as if this character paper was meant to be submitted to a local library. But my silent bliss turned out to be premature as several known party hawks raised their hands. Vadim gave the

THE FLIGHT

floor to one of them.

"I can't believe my ears," the man declared. "We're dealing here with a man who intends to betray his homeland, our beloved country which brought him up and gave him his education, his apartment, and free medical care for his family. It is our duty to ask him very hard questions first and then come back to this discussion." Two more like-minded communists out of fourteen members of the bureau who were present sounded their approval. The faces of the rest showed no emotion. A moment of grim silence followed.

Then Vadim spoke in a stern authoritative tone, "I must remind the comrades," he said, "that our party and government have, in principle, decided to allow persons of Jewish nationality to emigrate to Israel. We see no obstacles to emigration in this case. We all know that this document is just a formality. We must let him go anyway. And we've got several items on today's agenda to discuss. We must move on. Let's not waste precious time." And that was the end of it. I was thus spared the chambers by this remarkable man and got my first paper to emigrate relatively easily.

On the other hand, my wife did not have any such help on her side. Despite her repeated requests, local party bosses at her school would not issue a character paper

THE FLIGHT

to her. No one would even talk to her about it. There was nothing for us to do but to decide she quit her job and that our application would list her as unemployed. That's what the party bosses at her school wanted all along.

Of course, we still needed those other two papers - one from my wife's mother, and another, from mine. My mother-in-law was understandably upset at the news we were planning to leave since she loved her grandchildren very much. She did not want us to go, but she signed the paper with an objection. The remaining obstacle seemed insurmountable.

THE FLIGHT

Rosa seated, playing piano during Christmas festivities in preschool, Moscow 1967

THE FLIGHT

Katerina, Rosa and Katya at the dacha outside Moscow. Rosa is wearing the dress in which she later fled the country. Krasnaya Pahra, June, 1973

THE FLIGHT

Chapter Seven
Saved by a Dream

The end of April was upon us. I was constantly trying to find a way out of our predicament. I discussed it with close friends, and with Jewish activists at the Moscow synagogue. The prevailing advice was to write to the country's top leaders asking them to waive "the paper requirement" in my case. I listened silently and nodded my agreement, amazed at the naivete of my counselors.

I knew some Jews who had been in our same situation many months before, who had tried this approach. They were still waiting for a reply from Brezhnev and Co. Worse yet, those who had not been fired from their work found their situation shaky at best.

They and their families were often treated as traitors. Everyone was free to harm them emotionally and even physically; the authorities would react, well, to put it mildly, indifferently. It would have been plain stupid of us to join their ranks.

I also knew some Jews who had successfully left. Before leaving, one friend who had emigrated ahead

THE FLIGHT

of us mentioned that it may be possible to get to the U.S. from the required transit stop in Vienna, Austria, instead of going to Israel. America had been my dream for many years, so I asked him to please let me know if it was possible to buy tickets on a flight to the U.S. from Vienna. We agreed that if he got to Vienna and this was indeed possible, he would send me a postcard in code language stating, "*It's easy to buy tickets to the Opera in Vienna.*"

Because the KGB read the mail in the Soviet Union, such a "code" postcard would avoid raising unwanted attention. Educated Soviets knew the Opera in Vienna was world-renowned; this code phrase would slide under the radar of any mail inspection. A few months later, I received a postcard from my friend with these exact code words. Now I knew my family had a chance to make it to the U.S.

To make that happen, we needed a formal invitation from a U.S. citizen who could serve as our sponsor. Fortunately, we knew one person.

In July of 1968, my wife attended the baptism of her Godchild, Boris. At the baptism, she happened to meet a truly kind and generous Russian American, named Michael Zvorikin, who was visiting Moscow.

The Russian man expected to be the Godfather had not shown up. He was so drunk he could not get out of bed. Rather than postpone the baptism, my mother-in-law suggested the family ask one of the

THE FLIGHT

men at the church. Several Russian men declined but Michael, who was there praying, responded, "With Pleasure!"

After the baptism, Rosa kept in touch with Michael, so she wrote to him and asked if he would sponsor us. She explained that I spoke English and would be able to find a job. Gratefully, Michael responded, "With pleasure," and he sent us an invitation.

We would pretend to leave for Israel, the only place I was allowed to go as a Jew, but change direction once in Vienna, and go to the U.S. instead. Even thinking of such an opportunity was extremely exciting. But what on earth could I do? How could I outsmart the KGB about the paper my mother wouldn't sign and get us out?

The end of April in Moscow is usually a lovely season. After the harsh, frigid winter, it is such a relief to part with a heavy overcoat and hat and to go outdoors with just your jacket on. I remember one of those delightful spring days of 1973 as if it were yesterday.

I was strolling along a street at lunchtime, in the vicinity of our Institute, thinking about my problems, as usual. Deeply engrossed in my thoughts, I became unaware of what was going on around me. I ended up in the middle of an intersection surrounded by cars, jolted from my lethargy by the sound of screeching brakes. It was a close call that forced me back to reality.

THE FLIGHT

I hurried back to the office to get on with my duties.

That night I couldn't sleep. Several times, just as I was beginning to drift into subconsciousness, that scene at the intersection would repeat itself in my brain with striking intensity. The same screeching sound would give me a jolt. I would wake up in a cold sweat. Sleep finally came as dawn arrived.

The dream that followed was as real as the nightmares before it. I stood in a circle of friends who were asking me questions about my family's emigration status; I was telling them that it didn't look good. "I've got a very serious problem with my mother. She won't sign the paper required of parents, which is blocking our emigration."

One of them said, "I know what your problem is. Don't you know what to do? Just tell them that your mother is dead; you won't need any paper from her." Then the dream was over.

I woke up again with a jolt, but this time there was no sweat. There was a feeling that I'd just discovered something particularly important. I looked at my watch. It was ten minutes after six o'clock. Time to get up.

I knew, of course, that, to accept my application without my parents' papers, the Visa Office would want to see the parents' original death certificates.

THE FLIGHT

I had a death certificate for my father, the authorities had issued it to me in 1956, after Khruschchev's sudden admission about Stalin's massacres. At the time, my father was, as they said, *"posthumously exonerated."* The *Cause of Death* on the death certificate was left blank. The KGB women at the Visa office would, no doubt, know what it meant, and I surmised that would give them deep satisfaction.

I would also need to present a death certificate for my mother, who was still living, of course. It had been a few days since the friendly advice was given to me in my dream when a solution to this problem became crystal clear.

I had two close Jewish friends whose mothers had died, one after another, within the last year. I was sure that, if asked, either of them would give me his mother's original death certificate to file as my mother's, despite unpredictably dangerous consequences to himself in case the scheme would somehow blow up in our faces.

I knew my friends well enough. Neither of them hesitated for a second, and one of them, Victor, brought me the document needed the next day. His deceased mother's last name was not mine, of course, but neither was my mother's. It did not matter; since the early 20's many women in the Soviet Union routinely carried their maiden names into marriage, so I did not expect any trouble from this direction.

THE FLIGHT

What gave me pause, though, was the possibility that I might be asked to produce my own birth certificate, in which the names of both parents were always listed. If this were to happen, my newly acquired document would serve as direct evidence of forgery against the State. And then *The Soviet Power* would not need to stretch its law too much to put me in a "special car" on a train going East to Siberia. I realized I would need to spend some additional time researching KGB practices in this narrow field of documentation requirements for Jews asking to emigrate in the opposite direction, West.

So, after weeks of painful deliberation, anguish, and fear, I came to the only remaining question - does the Moscow Visa Office routinely ask an applicant to produce his birth certificate or does it not?

For the next three days, during its working hours, I stood at the door of the Moscow Visa Office leading to the room where people entered with their exit visa applications. It was always the same three women inspectors in the room accepting or rejecting the papers. By this time, the names and looks of each one, as well as their treatment of applicants, were a constant topic of discussion among Moscow Jews.

One of the three women was a senior inspector. She was a tall, lanky, middle-aged woman. According to rumors, she was quite tolerant for her position, usually treating applicants in a calm, reasonable manner compared to the two other younger and much

THE FLIGHT

more abrasive ones. By some unexplained joke of bureaucratic fate, she had a last name, which in contemporary Russian sounded kind of biblical and clearly Jewish, although no one in his right mind would have taken her for a Jew. Not on this job, anyway. Still, a Jewish visa applicant who found himself at her desk could consider himself lucky.

Meanwhile, my task for the time being was to find out about the visa process. For those three days, I talked quietly to every applicant exiting the inspectors' room, asking him or her a prepared set of questions on their interview and its final result, such as, were the papers accepted or rejected, and, if rejected, why? I even met a few acquaintances of mine and had a chance to go into much greater detail with them.

Altogether I talked to about thirty applicants, both men and women. Not even one of them was required to produce his or her birth certificate. As for the other documents, both the official and unofficial requirements were generally confirmed, by my *exit poll,* to be what I had expected. Now I knew what I needed to do.

A postcard, which summoned me to the Moscow Visa Office to receive our exit visas, came in the mail on Saturday, August 18th, 1973.

I made a point to meet with my first daughter, Emma, who was eighteen at the time, to let her know our plan and say goodbye to her. And on Sunday, August 19th,

THE FLIGHT

Gertruda, Rosa's sister, came to visit. Rosa and Gertruda sat in our apartment chatting, and I went out to run some errands. Gertruda is a character; for example, upon learning about our desire to leave she had asked my wife to leave our daughter Katya in Moscow with her because we had two children, and she had none. Of course, we immediately declined.

As I left for my errands, I asked Rosa to please not use my typewriter. Rosa expressed interest in learning to use it, so I promised to teach her once we emigrated. We agreed she would not use it in the meantime, since it was such a precious commodity at the time. I returned more quickly than expected from my first errand to find Gertruda on my typewriter, against Rosa's wishes!

Gertruda and I got into a huge argument, and she kept egging me on. Finally, under the stress of the moment, I not-so-nicely asked her to leave. As she slammed the door she exclaimed, "You'll remember me!"

Never mind, I thought, *Focus on the task at hand.*

The next day was Monday, August 20th. I was at the Visa Office door by six in the morning. A dozen people were already there forming a line. I took my place in line; the Office opened its doors at nine. By that time there were about fifty of us in line; many of them carried their exit visa applications completely filled out. I did too.

THE FLIGHT

By now, because of my research, I had all the necessary information about how the visa process worked. It was clear to me that, if I could get through an interview with our papers accepted, the visas would be ours for the taking. The interview with the Office Inspector served as the only and final clearance. In the spring of 1973, thousands of application forms were being submitted in a short period. I figured it would have been impossible for the authorities to set up a routine procedure to carefully check the answers in each visa application, even for the overstaffed KGB apparatus.

My homework paid off. The interview (my lucky star led me over to the Senior Inspector's desk) was anticlimactic. When asked, I stated that both of my parents were dead, as I had written in answer to the application questions, and to the request of proof produced two original death certificates. The woman took the documents from me, carefully read them, and made some notes in my file; both certificates were on the same Government-prescribed and numbered form, exactly like federal forms in the U.S., with all columns (except one) duly filled out. Each bore the official seal of an appropriate Registrar's Office. The Senior Inspector didn't ask me any questions about my parents. I knew, though, that she wrote down the names. I didn't care. After a moment of silence, I was handed both documents back. Soon the interview was over. I received the precious exit visa papers at about 11:30 am.

THE FLIGHT

We had two full weeks to leave the country. It was more than enough time to complete the necessary preparations, ask for and be issued entry visas to Austria and Israel, buy Aeroflot tickets to Vienna, which would be a transit stop, exchange money, etc. We also made all the personal arrangements, chief among them was with Victor who, again as a devoted friend, agreed to take over my monthly financial donations to my mother.

There we were in the middle of the emigration commotion, an entirely new social phenomenon in Moscow, and I interacted with dozens of Jews. I always tried to find out what they thought they would do. At the time, most of them were still afraid to face the wind of freedom. It took guts to make up your mind quickly and to cut the umbilical cord. Some couldn't do it; they had grown up here and lived their settled lives. They knew the devil. Well, so did Jews who stayed under Nazis too long.

It looked like it might really happen for us, we would be one of those Jewish families who made it out.

As a Jew in the Soviet Union, religion, including Judaism, was forbidden. After all, the Soviet Power had *solved the problem* of all religions. Being a Jew, a Tartar, or an Eskimo was considered strictly a matter of one's ancestral origin or nationality. This mandatory denomination was entered by the Ministry of Internal Affairs into everyone's internal passport at the age of sixteen. This internal passport was used exclusively

THE FLIGHT

inside the country for identification as a means to inventory, divide, and rule almost two hundred and fifty million people. A separate passport was issued for international travel.

It seemed reasonable to wonder why the government would even care about my upbringing. As an orphan, like so many millions and millions of other children, we were brought up to adulthood without God but with the deafening drumbeat of constant cynical promises of an imminent paradise on Earth.

These promises were shamelessly gushed on our society by Kremlin proponents, yet meanwhile, everyone privy to real conditions in science and industry could tell horror stories about hours of incompetence, waste, and corruption. People were fed up with superficial and empty promises when, at the core, so much was wrong. So, in the end, it was not faith that inspired most Soviet Jews to flee.

Although many of them were eager to start a new life in Israel and to open themselves and their children to Jewish traditions and Judaism, others, among them many educated professionals and technocrats, were disgusted with the raging anti-Semitism in all echelons of power, with the pervasive suppression of freedom, and with lies and hypocrisy amid the universal dreariness of life.

These Jews just wanted out. To go west. To live in freedom. In a modern democratic civilization. To test

THE FLIGHT

their professional mettle. To improve their lot. But in 1973, which was the first year of mass Jewish emigration, their numbers were still statistically small.

We would go! As far as we could. We must, at least for the sake of the children. Brezhnev had set a door ajar, and America was taking us in. Only God knows how long this may last. Maybe it's now or never.

THE FLIGHT

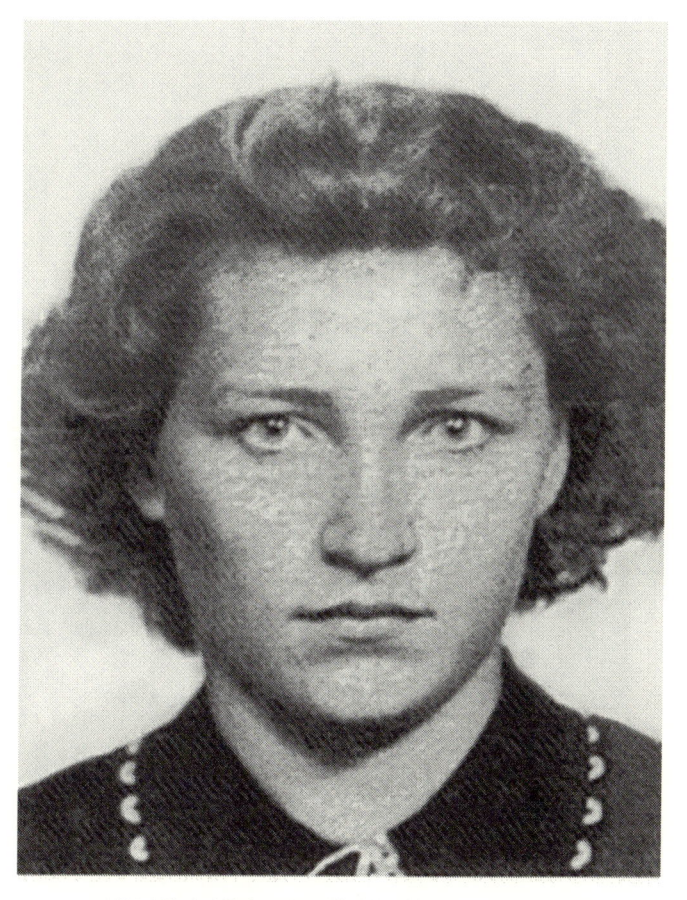

Gertruda, Rosa's sister, Moscow, circa 1956

THE FLIGHT

Gertruda, (left, Rosa's sister), Katerina,
(Rosa's mom), Rosa (right); Moscow, 1959

THE FLIGHT

Chapter Eight
The Subpoena

It was noon on a great summer day in Moscow, Monday, August 20th, 1973. There was no need to hurry. To this day, I cannot explain why I stopped a taxi the very moment I came out of the Moscow Visa Office Building and told the driver to go full speed to Arbat Square.

Arbat Square was the location of the Embassy of the Netherlands, which had represented the interests of the State of Israel in Moscow since June of 1967 when the Kremlin closed Israel's diplomatic mission in a fit of rage. I hurried in to request entry visas to Israel for my family.

A modest building, the Dutch Embassy was packed with Jews from Moscow and adjoining areas. They all had their exit visas and needed an additional stamp; permission to enter Israel. A Soviet Jew was not allowed to go anywhere else. An embassy official collected visas from everyone present. In a couple of hours, he handed them back to us.

The crowd swept outside and inundated the street.

THE FLIGHT

"Where's the Austrian Embassy?" someone asked. I did not hear an answer, but I knew exactly where it was. I saw the bus that could take me there coming to a stop on the other side of the street and sprinted to catch it.

It was almost 3 pm when I reached the gates of the Austrian Embassy. Only two people were in front of me. An embassy man came out and, in broken Russian, told the militiaman sitting in the booth, "These three are the last ones. Enough for today." In twenty minutes, I was out of the building with the Austrian stamps in our exit visas permitting us to enter Austria.

Now it was on to the bank to change money. Once we had been issued visas, the State allowed us to exchange rubles for up to four hundred American dollars. This service for emigrating Jews was only available in Moscow at one office of the State Bank, located far away from the Austrian Embassy. I could have gone there the next day, but the same subconscious alarm bell urged me not to put it off.

The bank was to close at 5 pm. It was 3:25, so I ran all four blocks to a Metro station nearby and kept running down the moving escalator, as the subway train was pulling up to the platform. Great! Thank the Soviet Power for working electricity at least.

By six in the evening, I was home. For the first time in her life Rosa, who had been tied up with our baby girl,

THE FLIGHT

had a chance to see American paper money. I had seen it for the first time at the bank, just an hour before. I was immensely proud of my day's achievements. "Well, dear," I remember telling her, "What do you think? All three visas and the money to boot. Not bad for one day. You really need to appreciate me more."

Little did I know what Gertruda had done after she had stormed out of our place that Sunday afternoon. My wife's sister, the only person Rosa had confided in about the falsified death certificate, had gotten so angry at me that she tried to undermine our painstakingly developed plan to emigrate. That Sunday, she jumped on the train to the countryside to convince their mother that she should not let Rosa leave the country with me.

Gertruda told their mom I had treated her awfully and was a terrible husband. She even let her know about the falsified documents as part of her argument against me and convinced her to go to the Moscow Visa Office and tell them about it. The two of them took the train into Moscow from the dacha on Monday, August 20[th,] and went straight to the Moscow Visa Office that afternoon. I had just left the same office earlier with our exit visas in hand.

The next morning, on Tuesday, August 21, I spent

THE FLIGHT

another two hours in line, this time at the Aeroflot ticket office. It was almost 11 am when I held in my hands four tickets to Vienna for Monday, August 27. The take-off was at 9 am. In just six days.

We still had enough time to sell Rosa's piano, accordion, and some furniture items so we could leave a "trust fund" to Victor for my mother, to give away the rest of our belongings to her relatives, to pack the necessities in four suitcases and bags to take on the plane, to cede our small apartment back to the cooperative, and to say farewell to our homeland, to our relatives, friends, and many well-wishers.

I was back home at noon. Rosa was busy packing the first suitcase with children's clothing. Beside her, our seven-month-old Katya was sleeping gracefully in her crib. She did look like an angel with her curly hair and rosy cheeks. I could have stared at her forever but quietly kissed her tiny hand, waved the Aeroflot tickets in the air, put them back in my pocket, and whispered to Rosa to give me something to eat. We went to the kitchen and stood there talking in low voices when I heard a knock on the door to the apartment.

When I opened the door, two uniformed militiamen were standing out in the hall.

THE FLIGHT

"Are you Lev Eduardovich Perlov?" they asked sternly.

"I am." The reply stuck in my throat for a moment.

"Here's a subpoena for you. You are to appear at the Moscow Visa Office tomorrow at 9 o'clock sharp. Room 12, second floor. Captain Sheleva wants to talk to you. She says an error was made in your exit visas, and they are invalid. You read the subpoena, please."

I took a postcard-like piece of paper in my hand and said, "Thank you, I will, I will," I closed the door and slowly went back to the living room. I had to sit down; my legs couldn't hold me. Rosa looked at me in horror.

"What happened," she asked, "who was at the door?" She had Katya in her hands, who had been roused by the knock at the door.

I read her the subpoena. She sat down too. "They've found out," she said, "someone squealed on us." Her hands went numb and fell to her side, almost dropping the baby.

"Yes, they have," I replied, "but who could have done that?"

For a few moments, we felt desperate. Completely, utterly helpless. We'd been caught. Oh, they will make

THE FLIGHT

us pay for this. *Well,* I thought to myself, *there's going to be a place for me in that special car going East to Siberia after all."*

Then Rosa said, "There must be something we can do. No point just sitting here and guessing."

I started thinking aloud, "Now, let's see," my temples began pulsating feverishly. "The plane to Vienna takes off three times a week at 9 am on Mondays, Wednesdays, and Fridays. Today is Tuesday. Gosh, they've got a plane tomorrow, at the same time Captain Sheleva will be waiting for me." Rosa and I agreed I would go back to the airport immediately and try to exchange the Aeroflot tickets for the next morning.

I ran to the street. It was 12:30 pm, and no taxis were in sight. I was boiling with impatience, cursing silently. *There's one coming, finally, thank God.* I stepped out onto the pavement and raised both arms in the air.

Twenty minutes later I entered the Aeroflot ticket office. The line had disappeared, and the office was empty. The same clerk who sold me the tickets less than two hours ago was sitting behind the same window. The other windows were all closed. I went up to her and put my visas and the tickets out on the

THE FLIGHT

counter. "You know, I just bought these tickets from you," I said firmly.

"Yes, I remember you," she acknowledged.

"Listen. We're ready to go, and our cooperative asked us to move out sooner, they need our apartment for a single mother with two kids who have no place." I gave her my best excuse for needing to leave sooner than expected.

"All right, all right, what do you want?" She seemed willing to be accommodating.

With all the confidence I could muster I proclaimed, "I want to exchange the tickets for tomorrow's flight."

"I don't know whether we've got any seats left. I'll go and check that out. Wait a couple of minutes." She stood up and went somewhere inside.

My heart sank. *What if there are no seats!? They'll eat us alive.* I had no doubt as to what was in store for me. *Hell, I am not the first one. And I won't be the last. People live over there, and I will have to as well somehow .... But Rosa.... Victor... the kids.... My little angels.... Please, God.* I closed my eyes.

"Well, we've got only three seats left on tomorrow's

THE FLIGHT

flight, but you need four, don't you?" The words sounded like they came from afar. Was someone asking me a question? Yes, the woman clerk was talking to me from her ticket window.

I snapped back to the moment, "It doesn't matter, three is enough. Our baby girl doesn't need a separate seat. Thank you very much." Is there really a God in Heaven?

She took my four tickets and gave me three new ones and the money for the fourth. "Have a happy flight," she said. I thanked her and I thought; *Oh, dear, you don't know how happy it's going to be, if only we make it onto it.*

I took the metro home. At midday, the cars are almost empty. I was sitting alone and thinking again. It looked as if we had a new chance to fly.

My mind was racing. It is true that Captain Sheleva may decide to call her colleagues at Sheremetevo airport, give them our names and visa numbers, and cancel the visas. But why would she want to do that today? Isn't she going to see me first thing in the morning? Besides, they gave me the visas just 24 hours ago. Who do they think we are? Acrobats? Don't we need a few days to get entry visas to two countries,

THE FLIGHT

to exchange rubles, to pack our things for the long journey? I comforted myself. Naturally, she wouldn't be calling anybody. There's no point in her doing that. I felt relieved, we're still alive and kicking. I could not know then that in America, they would call this "positive thinking."

From a booth in the metro, I made phone calls to Victor and my other friend Oscar, asking them to drop everything at work and come to my home right away. I didn't have to explain anything; they knew the moment they heard me talking. They showed up within an hour, and our troubleshooting session began.

First things first - I wrote Victor a letter of apology. A short letter in longhand:

Dear Victor,

I have attached to this letter your mother's death certificate, which I am now returning to you. I found it in your family photo album when you gave me the pictures to look at during my last visit with you. I needed the document desperately and I took it. Please forgive me. I know this was low of me but there's nothing I can do about it now.

THE FLIGHT

I signed the letter and wrote the next day's date, August 22, 1973, under my signature. Then I put the letter and the death certificate into an envelope, stuck a stamp to it, sealed it, and wrote his home address.

"Put this in your deepest pocket," I said, giving Victor the envelope. "You'll drop it in a mailbox as soon as we take off tomorrow if we do."

Oscar, a criminal attorney, well known in Moscow's bar for his ability to twist almost any evidence in his client's favor, added with a smile; "And if they do, and if later anyone will tell you that this letter is a sham, never, ever admit that it is. Just say no, no, no, the letter is for real and repeat it in their face as many times as it will take for them to give up on you. That is if you don't want to see the sky in black squares," my dear friend Oscar said half-joking. (Seeing the sky in black squares is a Russian expression, which means looking out at the sky through prison bars on a window.) He couldn't foresee at the moment how precious this advice would turn out to be for Victor.

Our immediate problem now was my five-year-old daughter Sofia. More precisely, it was her absence. For the last couple of months, she'd been staying with Rosa's mother and sister, about sixty kilometers from the city. I'd have to get a taxi, go there that night, and

THE FLIGHT

bring her back without any hint of revealing to her grandmother why I was doing it.

Rosa couldn't go with me. She had Katya on her hands, and at least two more suitcases to pack. I knew this task would be anything but simple. My mother-in-law loved Sofia, her first grandchild, with a passion, she was one obsessed babushka. She wouldn't let her go from under her wing without an utterly convincing spin on my part. I was afraid of the task and did not hesitate to admit it. Rosa shared my fears.

After some more discussion, Oscar offered to go with me. I gratefully accepted. We planned to hire a taxi beforehand and, after the trip, hold it until the early morning hours, when we were to leave for the airport. That was not so simple either. Taxi drivers in Moscow, as everywhere, are a whimsical lot, and many might hate driving to your destination and/or sitting and waiting in the car, even for good money.

While we were talking, the afternoon weather suddenly changed. The sky grew dark, a strong wind blew open a window. I plugged in the radio; yes, a severe storm was approaching the area around Moscow. That's just what we needed, a potentially delayed take-off tomorrow. Or even flight cancellation. A new scare. My wife and friends tried to

THE FLIGHT

calm me down. In the tiny kitchen, Rosa served an improvised meal. We ate quickly amid the growing tension of the ticking clock.

THE FLIGHT

Oscar, Lev's friend who helped him escape,
Moscow, circa 1973

THE FLIGHT

Katerina, Rosa's mother at the dacha outside of Moscow, Krasnaya Pahra, Summer, 1973

THE FLIGHT

Chapter Nine
Leaving On A Jet Plane

The start of our trip out of town that evening was accompanied by a most violent outburst of nature. Oscar and I were able to hop in a taxi just as the world around us went mad; huge zigzags of lightning crossed the blackened sky in every direction followed by cosmic explosions of thunder. Rain came in like a wall of water. It seemed that Satan himself was giving a warning to all living creatures that the end was near. And in my situation, I couldn't help but take it personally.

Meanwhile, the taxi driver refused to drive anywhere in the weather, and, upon learning about our destination point, demanded that we get out. "Are you people crazy?" he said. "I'd never drive there even in good weather." We didn't budge. There was nowhere to go.

Some twenty minutes passed as we haggled with our host. The rain had let up a bit but was still pouring hard. We asked the driver to name his price for the trip. He named one ridiculously high. We declined.

He repeated his demand that we get out and then

THE FLIGHT

started swearing at us in Russian curse words, that ubiquitous lingo sprawling out of prisons and army barracks and famous for its wild indecency.

Oscar seemed to have been waiting for such behavior, the underworld subculture long being a part of his professional life as a criminal lawyer. In a nasty guttural tone of voice, he asked the driver how long it had been since he was in trouble with the law and whether he was looking for trouble again. *At least that was his point, as I understood it*. Then he threw at him a dozen names from both sides of recent Moscow law enforcement investigations of some corrupt taxi drivers. Oscar mentioned the sentences they had received, leaving no doubt in this driver's mind which side he himself came from.

The poor fellow deflated like a spiked balloon, humbly muttered his agreement to drive where he was told to and be paid by the meter. Boy, I was glad to have my friend Oscar with me!

It took us almost two hours to get to the "dacha"; two small rooms in a wooden cottage that had been leased by a Moscow kindergarten to its personnel for the summer. My sister-in-law, Gertruda, worked for a kindergarten as a music teacher. The kindergarten children were quartered nearby.

It was past eight o'clock when Oscar and I went inside. My mother-in-law, Katerina, was reading Sofia a fairy tale, getting ready to tuck her in. Katerina, of course,

THE FLIGHT

didn't expect to see me (Oscar remained in the outer room) and, being caught off guard, just stared at me without saying anything.

I had prepared a ruse during our taxi ride. I told her that prophylactic shots were required of all who were to travel abroad, and that all members of my family were scheduled for the procedure at 7:30 am the next day. "I came in a taxi hired by a friend," I explained. "I have to take Sofia with me, but I'll bring her back by noon tomorrow."

My mother-in-law, like most of my fellow citizens at the time, wouldn't think of questioning what was required by the authorities. She realized that she had to let the child go. But it took only seconds for her to decide to join us.

Well, I was ready for this one too. "I am sorry ma'am," I said, "but it is Oscar who's in charge of transportation and he has to pick up two other people on the way to the city. There's just no place in the car for you. There was nothing else she could do but to give her granddaughter, her priceless treasure, her last goodbye kiss.

Yes, I was being cruel to her, and I hated myself for it, but we all lived in a cruel world.

I held my dear Sofie as she slept in the back seat of the car all the way back to the place we called home, maybe for one more night. Holding her hand I watched

THE FLIGHT

her sleep; I might have closed my eyes and relaxed if I could just stop thinking of tomorrow. The relentless rain kept pouring.

We had to let this driver go, of course, and not in front of our apartment house. At least one block away. Any unfriendly witness to our flight in the morning might turn out to be dangerous, although we had no clue of how or why. But better be safe.

Everything was all right at home. Rosa was busy packing and deciding what to bring and what to leave behind. For herself, she packed nothing, only the navy blue, polka dot dress she had handmade and would wear on the flight.

Since we did not have a phone at home, Victor had already been down to a street phone to call home and tell his wife that he would be back home in the morning. Oscar did the same. The children soon went to sleep, and the four of us sat down in the kitchen for a late supper.

We needed to decide what we would do in case the morning flight was delayed due to the weather. None of us dared to talk about the potential of a flight cancellation; it was better not to think of it at all. Victor, who had listened to the radio, assured us that, according to the forecast, the weather would improve. That gave me some hope.

After a brief discussion, we produced a brilliant idea.

THE FLIGHT

If between 9 and 10:00 AM the plane was still on the ground, Oscar would call Captain Sheleva pretending to be me. He would tell her that his infant had come down with a fever and he needed to take her to the clinic. He would be at her office at 11:00 sharp.

We liked the plan. It could give us an extra couple of hours of priceless time and ensure our plane had cleared Soviet airspace. Now we needed to relax and get at least a few hours of rest. I looked at my watch, it was 11:15 PM. It was still raining hard outside the balcony door. There was no way to know what tomorrow would hold for us, only time would tell.

I woke up just as dawn started lighting the windows, I got up and went straight on the balcony of our tenth-floor apartment. The rain had stopped; the sky seemed in a mood to brighten; it was still too dark to be sure, but the early birds' chirping in the trees below was a hopeful sign.

"Thank you, God, thank you," I sighed looking up. I felt like a good soldier before a battle - *okay, let's get to it and see how it turns out*.

We realized that we would need more than one taxi for all of us plus our luggage. Victor and Oscar went to secure them for us. Some twenty minutes later Victor rode back in one. Our house belonged to my institute's cooperative which employed a doorwoman, and she had the key to the elevator. We had to wake her up so we could get the luggage down to the street. Our

THE FLIGHT

three suitcases (one full of my books and dictionaries plus two bags) came down just as Oscar pulled up in a second taxi.

Half an hour later Rosa emerged from the elevator with the kids. Katya slept blissfully in her arms, and Sofia, beautifully dressed and groomed, was looking at the two cars and the commotion at the entrance with her eyes wide open. She had just seen her mother lock up their apartment and then give the keys to Victor. She heard us almost whispering to one another in short rapid sentences and by now she knew that something unusual was going on. She didn't ask any questions, just watched.

Suddenly the door woman appeared, surprising us all. "My, my, where is it that you're all heading to at such an early hour?"

We looked at each other dumbstruck, not knowing what to tell her without revealing too much information, and Sofia exclaimed, "To Babushka's! To the dacha!"

We went back to the task at hand, trying to suppress our laughter. The morning bloomed, with hope. It was a splendid morning indeed. By seven o'clock we stood in the lengthy line of passengers at the security checkpoint of Sheremetyevo International Airport.

Most people around us were Jewish emigrants on the same flight to Vienna. The line was moving

THE FLIGHT

excruciatingly slowly. The customs, we already knew, never let Jews get out easily. I was not afraid of the luggage inspection, even if I wanted to take something out surreptitiously, I couldn't possibly take an additional risk. I found out only later that Rosa had snuck a gold ring with a diamond and two rubies that her father had given to her mother into our daughter's bottle of yogurt so that the airport security would not take it. Airport security confiscated all valuables. Her mother had given her the ring for a "rainy day". It's a good thing I didn't know about the ring.

My one and only fear was the visas; we prayed that we would get to the checkpoint before nine so that "*our captain*" would still be waiting for me in her office. It was clear now that the plane would not take off by 9:00 or shortly after as planned.

Rosa sat with the kids in a row of chairs by the wall, doing her best to restrain Sofia, who was getting tired of waiting. My friends stood in line with me trying to keep me calm. The closer we came to the checkpoint, the harder they tried.

Fifteen minutes to nine, it was finally our turn. Victor and Oscar hugged and kissed us. "Don't forget about the letter," I whispered to Victor. I couldn't say anything else. I felt a lump in my throat, and there were tears in my eyes.

They stepped aside; I looked at Oscar for the last time and, to remind him to call Sheleva, made a revolving

THE FLIGHT

motion with my fist around my ear. He gave me a smile and a nod.

The next moment we were up on a checkpoint podium. I gave our visas to the border guard and stared at his face. He looked down, studied our pictures, and then stared at us, "Two children?" he asked. Breathless, all Rosa and I could do was nod in unison. He checked the visas again. "All right," he said, giving them back to me, "Move on to customs please." And he waved his hand.

We took our last steps behind the "Iron Curtain" and with the wave of a hand, we were cut off from our previous life. From our most devoted friends, from so many people and places we knew so well and cherished so dearly. Customs were mean, slow, and suspicious, but we let them indulge themselves one last time. There was no turning back now, silent, and with patience we crossed to the other side.

The plane's engines roared for take-off at ten eighteen. We were sure Oscar had made his phone call by now. My wife was joyful and relieved when we took off, but I warned her that they could still turn the plane around and told her, "Let's not rejoice until we land in Vienna." We would be flying in Soviet air space for more than two and a half hours; we kept wondering if they would land the plane because of us. Since there were some foreigners on board, we guessed it would be too much trouble.

THE FLIGHT

At last, we exited the plane in Vienna, and we hurried across the tarmac to the unknown. To the rest of our lives, to new, entirely different trials, to everything that freedom would bring us.

THE FLIGHT

THE FLIGHT

Michael G. Zvorikin, April 1969, who sponsored
our family to come to the USA

Opera in Vienna. Lev's friend sent him a postcard stating "It's easy to buy tickets to the opera in Vienna" to inform him he could get to the US once in Vienna

THE FLIGHT

Chapter Ten
Brave New World

In Vienna, we were given temporary housing in a communal apartment that we shared with two other families in the same situation.

Sofia had outgrown her sandals and was complaining that they were uncomfortable, so we went shopping in search of new shoes for her. My wife was amazed at how carefully the Italian shoe salesmen measured Sofia's feet, gave her a mirror, and fitted her with new, Italian sandals. We had never experienced anything like it.

Afterward, we found a park for her to play in while Katya slept in the stroller. Rosa and I sat down on a bench, and knowing we had barely made it out of the U.S.S.R., she began to weep in relief. Through her tears, she kept asking, "Who betrayed us?"

A week later, having overcome my apprehensions, I made an international night phone call to Victor. He did have a telephone at home, but I expected he would be too afraid to talk. Nothing in his voice

THE FLIGHT

indicated he was hesitant to talk, and he was glad to hear from me. He couldn't tell me any details, of course, but I learned the reason behind our precipitated departure.

That's when we found out that on August 20th (the morning I had visited the Visa office) late in the afternoon my mother-in-law showed up at the Visa office to find out whether my mother had agreed to let us go. To her surprise, no doubt, the official asked, "His mother isn't dead, is she?" The poor woman answered, "No."

A routine police state reaction followed. Every citizen lived in fear of a police subpoena and understood that obedience was expected.

I also learned the call Oscar made on my behalf to Captain Sheleva, about an hour before we were airborne, had the desired effect and she waited for my arrival until noon. By 2 p.m., when our plane was approaching Vienna, she had arrived at our apartment with two militiamen.

Victor was in the apartment still packing up all the things we had left behind when she arrived. She asked if he was Perlov.

He said, "No, I am Ginsburg" and she said, "We want

THE FLIGHT

to talk to you too. Where is Perlov?"

"He has flown off," Victor replied.

"How has he flown off?" she exclaimed in disbelief.

Eventually, we would find out even more details about who betrayed us.

Rosa kept in touch with her mother through letters, and after a couple of years she finally asked her mom, "Do you know who betrayed us?" Her mother wrote back and told her the whole story.

"It was your own sister who betrayed you. I beseech you to please forgive her," Rosa's mother begged in her letter.

In the Spring of 1989, Victor visited us in the U.S., and we heard the rest of his story. The KGB found out that it was his mother's death certificate that I had used, and they tormented him regularly for three years, trying to make him an informer, *or else*.

He read them my letter, which had arrived by mail and stood fast against all accusations and extortion, never deviating from Oscar's advice. He never told them who called Captain Sheleva that morning, insisting it must have been me. They tried to pin it on him, of course. They could not disprove anything he said and

THE FLIGHT

eventually had to leave him alone.

At the time, we had no idea about any of it. We stayed in Vienna for two weeks where we were finally able to redirect our plans and process our emigration to the United States. We had our formal invitation from a sponsor in the U.S., Michael Zvorikin, at the ready.

After our two weeks in Vienna, we were sent to Rome for two months while en route to the U.S. There, in September of 1973, we met a Jewish family who had just arrived from Moscow through Vienna. They told us that a birth certificate was now required from every Jew applying for an exit visa.

"Why is that," I asked?

"Well, the rumor has it that one very smart Jew, whose mother refused to sign the paper, declared she was dead and used someone else's death certificate to get the visa. We wonder if they caught up with him or if he got away with it!"

My wife and I laughed in disbelief and then told them the whole story, explaining we were the ones who had pulled it off. They could not believe it.

After a nearly two-month stay at the seaside resort of Lido di Ostia near Rome, and our delightful introduction to the Eternal City and the Vatican, we

THE FLIGHT

were filled with gratitude to the Italian people for their exceptionally warm welcome and hospitality.

The Italians treated us with great kindness, both because of their national temperament and tradition, and because we were going to live in the United States. As soon as they heard we were headed to America, they immediately showed us respect. It was September of 1973, and the entire world was impressed by the magical success of the Americans in space, crowned by their landing on the moon. Surely it was a near-fabulous place!

We arrived in New York on an Alitalia plane on October 25, 1973. The next day, we took a local flight to Minneapolis. We were the first Russian-Jewish immigrants of the new wave to arrive in that city.

For this reason, we were warmly welcomed at the airport by the leaders of the local Jewish family assistance service. An apartment had already been prepared for us, and it seemed that there would be no significant problems. However, on the way from the airport, I was told in the car that there was no job for me in Minneapolis. I didn't know what to be more upset about, this fact or the rudeness of the representative of the Jewish charity. Of course, I immediately began to regret that I had chosen this city

THE FLIGHT

rather than New York, for example.

We chose this place because I had heard a lot about the summer heat almost all over the United States and decided to choose a climate similar to Moscow's. My wife and I just hate the heat. But we realized shortly after our arrival that climate was last on our list of worries, and the decision to go to Minneapolis turned out to be a mistake. I was now geographically distant from the East Coast, where my potential employers were located.

We stayed in Minneapolis for about a year. I worked there for a couple of months in a construction firm as an estimator (the owner was a Jew and he hired me personally) but, having earned unemployment benefits from the state of Minnesota, I soon quit the job.

The working conditions there were inhumane, not to mention the poor pay. Six employees sat at their own tables in a room of about sixteen square meters, with a ceiling less than two and a half meters high and sealed windows that could not be opened. Four of them smoked non-stop, which was allowed at that time. I had to work without a minute break, and I was paid three dollars and forty cents an hour, which was barely enough for my family to eat. How could I not

THE FLIGHT

recall Marx with his theory of surplus value and free Soviet labor?

I didn't like it at once, and I gave up this "work" under the threat of an inevitable heart attack. Since I still wanted to live, I had no other choice. The reaction of Jewish charity workers to my decision was sharply negative: *That ungrateful Jew...* But they had to continue to pay for my apartment since I had two small children.

I gradually became unconcerned. I was now thinking only about surviving. My unemployment benefits were almost as much as my former "paycheck" and for the next few months, the state of Minnesota gave me food coupons that allowed us to buy food at a significant discount. In short, we were now living like the "average" American poor. But I was determined not to stay on welfare.

I soon passed the state exam for a real estate salesman's license and joined a firm that sold building lots in one of the states in the West. This firm paid no salaries, only sales commissions.

As you might expect, I was not a salesman, so I had to re-qualify as an interpreter. After seeing an advertisement in the library for positions at the Voice of America, I passed a special exam which required

THE FLIGHT

translating texts about various topics (sports, art, politics, etc.) from English into Russian for six hours one day and then Russian to English for six hours the next day. I received a score of 478/500 and was then invited to work for the Voice of America in Washington, D.C.

We flew to Washington on September 18, 1974. I remember that as we walked outside, we were unpleasantly struck by the heat and humidity and talked about it with the Voice of America employee who met us. He laughed, "Is this a heat wave, you ask? The heat season is already over. Wait until next July."

Despite the challenges of our first year, I remember my great love for this country that so graciously welcomed us, my pride that my family and I would become its citizens, and my desire to do everything in my power for its prosperity and greatness.

THE FLIGHT

Rosa and Katya, Minneapolis, 1974

THE FLIGHT

Lev graduates with Masters' in Law, Georgetown, Washington DC, 1977

THE FLIGHT

Conclusion

By Katy G. Meilleur
(Katya)

My father worked at the Russian Service of the Voice of America (VOA) for twenty years, until he retired in 1994. He served as an editor and broadcaster of Western news to Soviets behind the Iron Curtain. Due to the nature of our escape, he changed his name whenever he went on the air so that he could not be identified in the U.S.S.R.

I know he put in the work to provide for our family, but I believe he also did it because he believed in democracy and freedom. Especially in the beginning, he often worked the night shift. I remember as a child having to tiptoe around the house quietly while he was sleeping during the day. My mom was always eyeing my every move. Waking him was a big no-no!

In the mid-1970s, my parents applied for citizenship by naturalization for our entire family. It came to my father's attention that the naturalization process for Russian immigrants took eight years. This was three years longer than the five-year process required for immigrants to the U.S. from all other countries.

My father decided to raise this issue with our Maryland congressman. My mother recalls that my father went to his office and met with him face to face to ask him, "Why do immigrants from the Soviet Union

THE FLIGHT

have to wait three years longer than all other immigrants to obtain their naturalization? I think this may be discriminatory."

The congressman responded, "Mr. Perlov, you're absolutely right. I will raise this issue in Congress and see what I can do." Sure enough, it was rectified. I guess every Russian in Maryland who has applied for naturalization has my dad to thank that the process takes five years rather than eight!

We were naturalized after six years, and in 1979, we hosted a party to celebrate with our new friends at our townhouse in Silver Spring, MD.

During this season in life, in 1977, my father also completed a master's degree in law from Georgetown University. He did this at the age of fifty, in a second language, with two small children, while working full-time at the VOA, within 4 years of escaping to a new country from communism!

In 1981, my father's friend, Oscar, immigrated to New York City from Moscow with his wife and son. That December, my father turned 55 years old, and we reunited to celebrate his birthday. It was a momentous occasion for all.

Later, my father's friend, Victor, and my half-sister, Emma, visited us in 1989. In this incredible reunion, we learned more details of their sides of the story. Victor had been threatened by the authorities for

THE FLIGHT

years due to the implications of his mother's death certificate, but he never gave in.

Emma had been officially adopted by her stepfather, who was a wonderful father to her. Victor eventually emigrated to Israel, where I visited him and his wife in 2000 and thanked them for their sacrifices on our behalf. To give you an idea of the incredible person Victor was, he moved to Israel in his 60's. He then contributed to his new country in his professional field, architecture. He was honored in Israel for his contributions by having his image placed on a postage stamp. In the stamp, he is wearing a shirt my dad had sent him as part of a thank you gift for watching over my father's mother after we left the U.S.S.R.

As for my father, neither the work at the VOA nor the hours there were easy. His time at the VOA from 1974-1994 was fraught with challenges. He was of course more fluent in Russian than English, but he had also studied English independently for years and was skilled at languages in general. In contrast, many of the people with whom he worked, including his supervisors, were immigrants or children of immigrants from displaced persons camps in Europe after World War II. This meant their Russian language was further removed, as was their experience, if any, of what life was like under Communist rule.

I remember my father telling me that, during this period, Solzhenitsyn, spoke publicly in the States about the Russian Service of the Voice of America.

THE FLIGHT

Solzhenitsyn said the VOA was broadcasting "nonsense" to the Soviet people, who were hungry for truthful information. (My father said the American translator for Solzhenitsyn translated it perfectly as 'inconsequential drivel'). Throughout the 20 years he worked there, my father often lamented what was being written and broadcast there.

He wrote of his experience, "I remember how in the fall of 1974, during a newscast, I was suddenly brought into the studio and handed a newly written news story to read. It was incoherent gibberish, a set of incompatible and uncoordinated words, riddled with grammatical errors, only remotely resembling the Russian language. I was a new employee at the time and in an effort to *uphold the honor of the company*, while reading, I was sweating profusely and painfully struggled to make something understandable out of this "nonsense" for broadcasting. As I left the studio, I approached the author and asked him if he had read his news after he had written it.

"What's the matter?" he asked.

"'The matter is," I replied, "that it was complete drivel."

He replied in disgust, "Why do you care so much?"

I cannot imagine how my dad felt being asked that question. Of course, he would immediately think of his experiences under Stalin, his father, and all the dear

THE FLIGHT

friends and family we left behind - Emma, my grandmothers, Oscar, and their families... Victor, who had risked his life for us.

My dad cared because those people yearned for and deserved quality newscasting to counter the communist propaganda they were constantly hearing, propaganda about how the West was less advanced scientifically, politically, and culturally than the Soviet Union. He cared deeply about the ideals of democracy and freedom for many more Soviets as well.

He was shocked that this was not taken seriously nor rectified by the leadership in the VOA. The longer he stayed at the VOA, the more he fought for competency in leadership, editing, and broadcasting. However, no one was removed from their post.

Of this, he wrote, "Speaking of *removal from the post*. I can't help but note that in my 20 years in government, I have never heard of this happening to anyone who foolishly, carelessly, maliciously, or out of criminal intent, failed in their duties, or abused their authority. It is quite another matter if a soccer (or basketball, or any sports) coach, at any level, fails to get satisfactory results for his team by the end of the soccer season. This one will be kicked out mercilessly and immediately because no blunders are acceptable here. Sport is our only serious and important activity and not foreign or internal politics."

Unfortunately, this struggle consumed his work life,

THE FLIGHT

and he became angry and embittered about the VOA and specific aspects of the American government. My dad eventually came to see that no country is perfect. He would cynically joke about his "final emigration", meaning death. But deep down he dreaded dying, as we all do at some level. I often prayed for him because I came to believe in Jesus as the Messiah in 1991. The verses I specifically prayed were from the Book of Hebrews in the New Testament: "[Jesus] too shared in their humanity so that by his death he might destroy him who holds the power of death that is, the devil and free those who all their lives were held in slavery by their fear of death. For surely it is not angels he helps, but Abraham's descendants."

Finally, the Berlin Wall fell in 1989, followed by the collapse of the Soviet Union in 1991. Both events were brilliant, much-needed rays of hope for all after the Cold War.

I will never forget the experience of going back to Russia for the first time as a family after the fall of communism. In 1997, Moscow celebrated its 850th anniversary. My whole family flew to see our relatives for the first time in 24 years to celebrate with them.

Unfortunately, both of my grandmothers passed away in 1986. However, my mother had forgiven her sister as her mom had beseeched her to do. We met Gertruda, their brother, and their families. We also met my dad's two half-sisters, Louisa, and Lora, and their families. Their mother had returned from the

THE FLIGHT

GULAG in 1948 after being there 8 years but had passed away in 1992.

After first reuniting with family and close friends, one of the stops during the visit was my dad's last place of employment in Russia. Many of the same guys were there! After the initial recognition of who my dad was and excited greetings, one of his former colleagues exclaimed, "That was you on the radio, wasn't it?"

Later, my half-sister Emma told me her mother used to regularly close herself off in the bathroom to listen to our dad on the radio. Her second husband was a communist so she could not let on. She would hide in the bathroom and run the tap so that he could not hear the radio.

"What are you doing in the bathroom for so long?" he would ask.

"Oh, nothing, just washing up" she would respond. She could not let him know she was listening to Western news.

If these people were listening to my dad, perhaps many others were too. Who knows, maybe in some way, all of his hard work relaying well-written news from the Western free world contributed to the demise of communism.

THE FLIGHT

THE FLIGHT

Unknown soldiers and comrades, likely from First Moscow Specialty School of the Air Force, 1938

THE FLIGHT

Lora (LT) and Luiza (RT), after their father Edward was killed by Stalin in the Great Purge and their mother was sent to the ALZhIR labor camp, Moscow, circa 1939

THE FLIGHT

Lev, second from right, conscripted into aviation branch of military, circa 1947

THE FLIGHT

Rosa, Moscow, Circa 1960

THE FLIGHT

Rosa, Zvenigorod, west of Moscow, Circa 1961

THE FLIGHT

Katya, party at our home after naturalization in Silver Spring Maryland, 1979

THE FLIGHT

Oscar, Katya, and Oscar's son, Vladimir, reunited in Washington, D.C., 1981

THE FLIGHT

Oscar and his wife, Zina, reunited with our family in Washington, D.C., 1981

THE FLIGHT

Oscar visiting Lev
Maryland, 1984

THE FLIGHT

Lev in his backyard with Emma, his daughter, and Victor, who helped him escape, Maryland, 1989

THE FLIGHT

Lev, Rosa and Victor, visiting Baltimore, 1989

THE FLIGHT

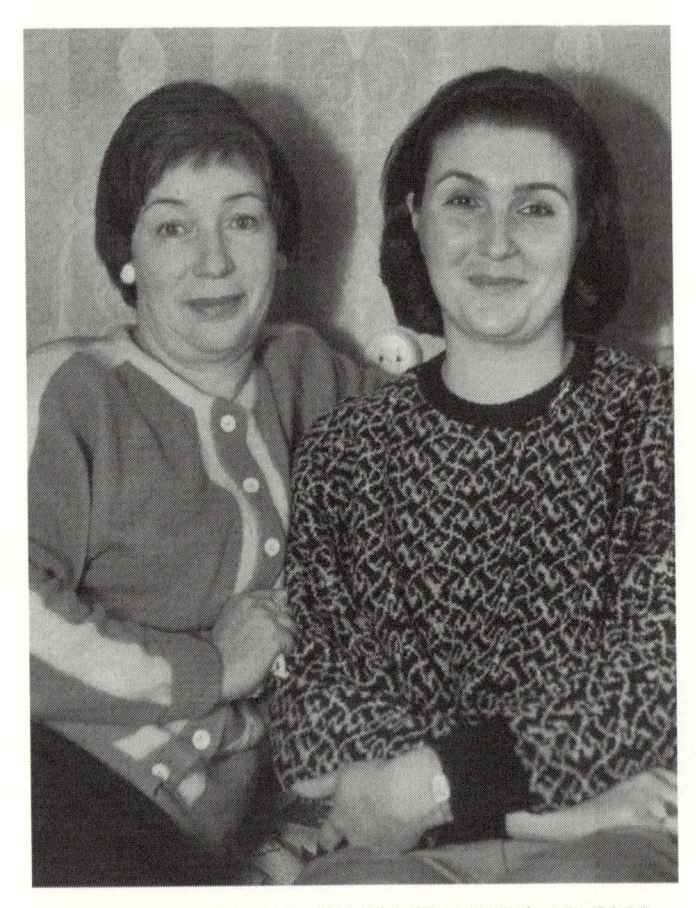

Lora, Lev's half sister, and daughter Natalya in 1989,
Lev and Lora's families reunited in Moscow in 1997

THE FLIGHT

Rosa and Lev, in front of the meat and produce store where they originally met in 1967, Moscow, 1997

THE FLIGHT

Lev and his niece, Natalya, Lora's daughter,
Maryland, 1998

THE FLIGHT

Rosa and Lev, New Year's Eve,
Maryland, circa 1998

THE FLIGHT

Katya visiting Victor and his wife Sophie in Beit Shemesh, near Jerusalem, Israel, 2000

THE FLIGHT

Victor was honored on a stamp for his contributions to architecture in Israel after moving there in his 60's. Pictured in a shirt my dad had sent him as a thank you.

THE FLIGHT